Nature's Nightmare

Analyzing David Foster Wallace's *Oblivion*

Greg Carlisle

Sideshow Media Group Press
Los Angeles / Austin

Cover Design: Kyle Ware

SSMG Press
Los Angeles / Austin
www.sideshowmediagroup.com

ISBN-13: 978-0-9889305-1-3

First Edition
10 9 8 7 6 5 4 3 2 1

for Laurie,

Caroline, Piper, and Lila

Table of Contents

Introduction

Upon publication of his second novel *Infinite Jest* in 1996, David Foster Wallace began working on his next novel, *The Pale King*, which was published unfinished in 2011. A study of *Oblivion*, the collection of stories Wallace published in 2004 about midway between his last two novels, is essential for tracking how Wallace got from *Infinite Jest* to *The Pale King*: what thematic motifs and narrative techniques does he continue to use, and how do his characters evolve? If *Infinite Jest* documents symptoms of and a preliminary diagnosis for American societal angst and malaise and despair, and if *The Pale King* documents attempts to manage that condition to varying degrees of success; then *Oblivion* documents case studies that will lead Wallace to a more informed diagnosis and treatment plan. Soon after the publication of *Oblivion*, Wallace made the 2005 commencement speech, published as *This Is Water* in 2009, that addresses the conflicting tensions that Wallace also deemed the "Broad arcs" of *The Pale King*: "Paying attention [vs.] boredom" and "Being individual vs. being part of larger things" (*TPK* 545). Both tensions are extensively explored in *Oblivion*, the former in its earlier incarnation of consciousness vs. oblivion.

Josh Roiland's essay on Wallace's journalism (Roiland 25-52) keenly articulates the tension between consciousness and oblivion in Wallace's work. Roiland contrasts the moral imperative of Wallace's "extreme consciousness" with Nietzsche's idea of oblivion as a healthy, powerful "screening device" to protect consciousness from damaging extremes. Although oblivion is primarily defined as Nietzsche uses it—a state of unawareness or unconsciousness, oblivion is also synonymous (in the *Oxford American Writer's Thesaurus* for which

unaware – N.
vs.
hyperaware – w.

Oblivion = obscurity

Wallace was a contributing editor) with obscurity: "limbo, anonymity, nonexistence, nothingness, neglect, disregard" (*OAWT* 621). The oblivion with which Wallace is concerned in his fiction is far more resonant with this latter characterization and paradoxically often goes hand in hand with extreme consciousness, because extreme consciousness *Not sure the connection is substantiated* characterizes not only our other-directed attention to the world and the people around us but also our self-centered anxieties. Many characters in *Oblivion* are extremely attentive and/or self-conscious, but their activities often serve to distract them from what they don't want to think about. They bury or obscure what they want to neglect or disregard about themselves under layers of details or mental abstractions. This behavior, symptomatic of the American problem with which Wallace is concerned, often leads characters into stasis or limbo or to a crisis of identity. Hence the motto Wallace buries in the text of the last story in the collection: consciousness is nature's nightmare.

To adjust our self-centered "default setting" (*TIW* 44-5) such that we are able "to collect and organize the noise and agitation of the phenomenal world" (Roiland 28) in a positive way is relentlessly challenging. The difficulty in crafting realistic, interesting characters that can navigate the noise and agitation of the world, maintaining the moral imperative of attentiveness and resisting the temptation to succumb to boredom, may have contributed to Wallace's problems writing *The Pale King* even before his health began deteriorating. The degree to which a few of Wallace's characters in *The Pale King* are more successful than the characters in *Oblivion* at balancing the tension between consciousness and oblivion, between attention and boredom, is the degree to which they are able to resist the tendency to layer and obscure and neglect and disregard, to pay sustained present attention to concrete details

Greg Carlisle

and to other people, to minimize psychic abstraction and self-consciousness, to ride out the boredom that will eventually give way to bliss (*TPK* 546).

Oblivion is a testament to Wallace's maturation and sophistication and trajectory for continued growth as an artist: subtler than *Infinite Jest* but just as bold, exhibiting the qualities of searing honesty and humor that mark Wallace's signature work. Although *The Pale King* indeed confirms the limitless potential of Wallace's artistry had he lived, *Oblivion* stands as the last book of fiction he published in his lifetime.

THE STRUCTURE AND METHOD OF THIS BOOK

This book will summarize and comment on each of the eight stories in *Oblivion* section by section. In some cases Wallace has already divided his stories; in others I infer divisions. Throughout the book, I title the sections (using a phrase from the section except for the sections of "The Soul Is Not a Smithy") in an effort to infer essential ideas and themes succinctly. This methodical approach is necessary due to the rich density of Wallace's text. Every passage is significant and is analyzed in terms of four areas of critical interest: 1) interrelation of narrative form and content, 2) relation of content to the overall theme of oblivion, 3) recurring thematic motifs in Wallace's work, and 4) assessment of content in relation to *Infinite Jest* and *The Pale King*.

The sense of oblivion as a tendency to obscure is represented graphically for each story by a figure of concentric circles, which represent either nested levels in the story's structure or something that characters have buried that has surface-level consequences. The identification of recurring thematic motifs is based on the themes I identified in *Elegant Complexity*, my study of *Infinite Jest* (cf. Carlisle, *EC* 23). Throughout the book, page numbers refer to the text of

Oblivion unless otherwise indicated. Quoted material from *Oblivion* is usually only given a page reference if the quoted material is from a section other than the section analyzed. Ellipses to indicate omitted material are only used in the middle of quotations: you will not see ". . . and but so . . ." (unless the ellipses are Wallace's). The book concludes with a summary and an indexed list of works cited.

Mister Squishy

This first story is an in-depth exploration of the tension of "Being individual vs. being part of larger things" (*TPK* 545), a major concern of *The Pale King*. The compulsion to be both puts us in a kind of limbo, a tense state of indecision or confusion that makes us long for the relief of satiation or stupor, of oblivion. "Mister Squishy" is the brand name of snack cakes that provide the satiation of a sugar rush, but the term might also be used as a pejorative for an indecisive person.

1. Quote unquote Full-Access (pp. 3-8)

In the story's first section, the narrator establishes a sense of disorientation and obscured meaning by using language that implies transition or indecision and the jargon of product description and testing. After completing Individual Response Profiles (IRPs), members of a Focus Group have "reconvened" in "another" nineteenth-floor conference room (where beverages are "available to those who thought they might want them") to work together on a Group Response Data Summary (GRDS) after they receive "Full-Access background information" from their facilitator, whose smile has the quality of "some vague diffuse apology." The product being tested is *Felonies!*, a death-by-chocolate type snack meant to offer the consumer a moment of "adult autonomy" in the face of "health-conscious" pressures. The product is manufactured by the Mister Squishy Company, whose cartoonish brand icon connotes "delight, satiation, and rapacious desire all at the same time."

The source of disorientation and indecision in this story is tension between the desire for individual autonomy and meaning versus the support and anonymity of group membership. Complex hierarchies, secret observations, and nested tests are constructed to absorb (to make distant, obscure, and impersonal) the shock of betrayals and to eliminate surprises with respect to an individual's loyalties to a group or brand. Mister Squishy's parent company has hired Reesemeyer Shannon Belt Advertising to accumulate test-market data on a potential new Mister Squishy-brand product. R.S.B. in turn employs Team Δy, a market research firm they "had begun using almost exclusively," to collect data that R.S.B. can use to assure Mister Squishy's parent company that a product meant to appeal to individual sensibilities is purchased by large groups of people. The fourteen-member Focus Group described in this first section includes two Unintroduced Assistant Facilitators (UAFs), who in the facilitator's absence observe without influencing the other members of the group to "help round and flesh out the data." In addition to the overt test of the product with respect to Preference and Satisfaction, there is a covert, nested test, unknown to the civilian Focus Group members, that tracks the effect of "Full-Access manufacturing and marketing" information on the group's "perceptions of both the product and its corporate producer." Note that the Focus Group is not really getting Full-Access information, but rather "the putative Full-Access information" that the facilitator "was authorized to share" (p. 12). Convoluted hierarchies, secret agendas, and nested tests invoke confusion and an overload of choices in the Focus Group members, a state of oblivion akin to that of the average consumer.

All of the narrative threads of "Mister Squishy" are initiated in this opening section. As the story progresses, the threads of the facilitator's observations and fantasies, Team Δy's politics and practices (such as the use of UAFs), and the climber (a thread foreshadowed by Wallace's panning from the

Greg Carlisle

nineteenth-floor conference room to "the street far below" for one line on p. 5) will converge to a point of maximum tension as the Focus Group begins the process of completing its GRDS and crisis events loom.

2. BEHAVIORAL DETAILS (PP. 8-13)

In the next section, we learn the name of the facilitator, Terry Schmidt, who has "a natural eye for behavioral details" and observes specific individual characteristics of each person in the group, paradoxically reducing them to statistics and percentages useful for product testing. He observes even as he behaves "as though he were interacting in a lively and spontaneous way" with the Group, "trained by the requirements of what seemed to have turned out to be his profession." Schmidt's observations are interspersed with personal and behavioral details from his own life, including the fact that he keeps "his own private records" of data he gathers for Team Δy.

We want to be both anonymous group-members and autonomous individuals; but the fact that each of us cannot escape being a person keeps us from truly being a people. Darlene Lilly calls herself "a people person," which presumably means she is other-oriented; but her job, like Schmidt's, requires that her interaction with the people in the Focus Groups ultimately serves the needs of her employer (and therefore her personal needs) rather than the needs of the other people in the room. In our consumer-oriented society, our jobs (our financial needs) dictate our group loyalties, and we struggle to balance "civic duty" and "elective consumption." We want to be accepted as we define ourselves, like the Group member "who had back problems and understood the dignity with which he bore them to be an essential part of his character"; but often our signals are too personal to be interpreted by others, like the Group member who "wore sunglasses indoors in such a way as to make some unknown type of statement about himself." Our pretense of achieving group identity without navigating the communication problems and requirements of personal sacrifice attendant to that achievement breeds the dangerously self-absorbed attitudes of the three youngest group members, "consumers who have never once questioned their entitlement to satisfaction or meaning."

3. MANIPULATIVE OR EVEN ABUSIVE IN THE NAME OF DATA (PP. 13-19)

The narrator jolts the reader with a couple of surprises to begin the next sequence. A figure—whose pants, sweatshirt, and hood are blue and white (cf. the "familiar distinctive Mister Squishy navy-and-white design scheme," p. 5)—is climbing the building. And the narrator, who wears an "emetic prosthesis," speaks in first person as a character in the story. He is the "second UAF" (the "affectedly eccentric UAF" has already been introduced to the reader on p. 10) and has a backup copy of his "brief script for the GRDS caucus" hidden "just inside [his] sweater's sleeve" (Schmidt "mistakenly" (p. 50) believes a man in "blazer and turtleneck" is the second UAF). How does this first-person narrator know Terry Schmidt's most personal thoughts (like his fantasy about Darlene Lilly on p. 16)? Perhaps we are to assume the first-person narrator is Wallace fantasizing that he is interacting with his characters.

Terry Schmidt thinks of "the youngest men's faces" as having "the clean generic quality of products just off the factory floor." Schmidt's job requires him to consider those with whom he interacts simply as consumers of the product he is testing, more like products than people. Product-testing "could be extremely manipulative or even abusive in the name of data." Product testing is designed to lower the defenses and prey on the insecurities of those tested in order to retrieve honest data. The strategies described on p. 18 brought women in one Focus Group "to such an emotional state that truly invaluable data on how to pitch Cheer Xtra in terms of very deep maternal anxieties and conflicts emerged." Does our view of others as simply consumers from whom useful data might be extracted dehumanize them to the point that we feel our manipulation is okay? It's more complex than that, because Darlene Lilly is bothered by the fact that, unlike participants in psychological studies, participants in product testing studies are not debriefed, and yet she accepts this as part of her job. Presumably, the data is considered to be worth the cost, but Schmidt—who believes that "[s]ometimes little things make a difference" (p. 9) and that the "whole problem and project of descriptive statistics was discriminating between what made a difference and what did not" (p. 12)—also believes that the "Focus Groups made little difference in the long run," that "the only true test was real sales."

Schmidt's Focus Group will "go past lunch" by design, initiating symptoms that will cause the group's "game-faces" to "begin to slip." Why do we have guarded game-faces, and why do product testers manipulate participants rather than simply trust the participants' responses? Why does the fact that we, like the buildings of p. 13, are "all partly in one another's shadow" breed mistrust rather than camaraderie? Do our own dark self-interests (the Senior Research Director sexually harasses Mrs. (p. 15) Lilly, about whom Schmidt also fantasizes) make us insecure about and cause us to mistrust and fear the motives and potential hidden agendas of others? We need to belong, but we fear rejection or loss of control. We will purchase a "*HelpMe* Personal Sound Alarm," but fear asking another person for help even with something as impersonal as product testing. Schmidt believes what is important to consumers is "[w]hat they conceived themselves to be," which is both self-interested and a plea to be accepted by a group on one's own terms.

4. STRANGE AND PROTEAN ENTITIES (PP. 19-25)

We learn that the climber has "either reflective goggles or very odd and frightening eyes indeed." Terry Schmidt's means of manipulating his Focus Group into giving him honest data is to act as if he is not manipulating them, using strategies which include the seemingly-unplanned marker trick, seeming to pluck "an example at random," and rolling his eyes in pretend mockery of statistical jargon. Schmidt is extremely attentive to the group members (note that the parenthetical phrases in this section seem to be the first-person narrator qualifying Schmidt's assumptions), but the trust he is attempting to build is for the purpose of data extraction. Because we want to appear superior rather than vulnerable, our group connections are often founded not on a request for inclusion but on a shared exclusion, as the eye-contact on p. 24 seems to be.

Our need to belong to groups and the influence that individual group members can have on one another is exemplified by the phenomenon of fads: a chain reaction of influence that leads to mass consumption. Team Δy "sought always to anticipate and fuel these sudden proliferating movements in group choice," hence the GRDS. But groups are "strange and protean entities," with interactions so complex that we must use computers to model them, allowing us to make distant and abstract the unknowable, uncontrollable nature of the group dynamics that affect our desperate need to belong.

Greg Carlisle

5. PRIVATE LINES OF THOUGHT (PP. 25-34)

Throughout the story, Terry Schmidt has been able to indulge in "private lines of thought" even as he maintains his "clumsy mime of candid spontaneity" "with a breeziness he [does] not feel." Now, we get even deeper into the psyche of Terry Schmidt, who felt "somewhat sullied and implicated by the whole enterprise of contemporary marketing" and that "people he was just trying to talk as candidly as possible to ["in his career" and "in his personal affairs", so presumably this does not include the Focus Group participants for whom he breezily mimes candidness] always believed he was making a sales pitch." Schmidt's feelings are given credence by the unfortunate circumstance and attendant cynicism of this truth: "legitimate concern for consumer wellbeing [i]s both emotionally and economically Good Business," a truth exemplified by the "tamperproof packaging in the wake of the Tylenol poisonings."

Schmidt's failure to actuate or even continue to believe in his idealistic fantasies of himself leads him down very dark paths indeed. A relatively innocent wish to open his heart to Darlene Lilly (although she is a married woman) leads to a fear of seeming creepily obsessed, which leads to Schmidt's actually being creepily obsessed on p. 26. Learning that his Tylenol-inspired professional fantasies of making a difference "were not in the main all that unique" leads him to view those fantasies as puerile and narcissistic (and to consider himself isolated from rather than united with all the other non-unique fantasists) which leads him to consider the option of making "a dark difference" by poisoning snack cakes in grand Tylenol fashion.

The ideal of "true marriage, meaning not just a ceremony and financial merger but a true communion of souls," seems miraculous and unattainable to Schmidt, who sees the people "in the conference room as like icebergs and/or floes, only the sharp caps showing, unknown and -knowable to one another." He sees himself as "100% average and unremarkable," associating his face with Mister Squishy's, "crude and line-drawn and clever in a small way, a design that someone might find some small selfish use for but could never love or hate or ever care to truly even know."

The group below watching the climber is also a "strange and protean" entity and a gathering of guarded, isolated individuals. Note that the climber "looked to be purposely idling, timing out his ascent to conform to some schedule," and recall that the first-person narrator is monitoring "both Real Time and Mission Time" (p. 14).

6. BRILLIANTLY MANAGED STRESS (PP. 34-42)

So far, each section of the story has focused primarily on Terry Schmidt with perhaps a paragraph devoted to the climber and the crowd outside. Now Wallace, "in opposition to the overall trend" of his narrative, focuses the entire section on the climber and watching crowd with only a single paragraph concerning Schmidt, who explains the phenomenon of Antitrends or Shadow Markets, in which (for example) a "Shadow snack simply worked to define itself in opposition to the overall trend" toward healthy snacks and against junk food. This story is primarily about the "stresses on individual consumers [i.e., people] caught between their natural God-given herd instincts and their deep fear of sacrificing their natural God-given identities as individuals, and about the way these stresses [a]re tweaked and-slash-or soothed by skillfully engineered trends." Shadow marketing for products like *Felonies!* "aimed to remind the consumer that he was at root an individual" and "not a mere herd animal," although he or she is of course both.

 Competing impulses toward both individualism and group membership can lead to a state of meta-awareness:

Greg Carlisle

complex, layered, self-conscious thought which breeds indecision or stasis and secretiveness or guarded attitudes. This section features several examples of nested complexity in which a thought or action is found to "spin inside and against the larger spin" of a higher-level thought or action. Schmidt makes a remark that he knows is controversial, but his pretended ignorance of the controversy will force his superior, Robert Awad (harasser of Lilly), to pretend that Schmidt really was ignorant and to speak with Schmidt "without unduly damaging Schmidt's morale over the putative boner, and so on" in a nested loop or secret game analogous the nested test currently being conducted by Awad on Schmidt and the other facilitators. The pager that goes off by prearrangement on Schmidt's cue and Schmidt's subsequent pretense of chuckling are similar games. The "whole industry seminar business" is a game of "marketing truisms to marketers."

In an example of both self-reflexivity and secrecy, some people in the crowd can't "resist looking at their own and the whole collective's reflection in the Gap's display window," but unknown to the crowd, "there was in turn a growing collection of shoppers inside looking out at them" through tinted glass. Those who call for the climber to jump are not jaded but "self-ironic," "simply parodying the typical cry of jaded onlookers." The "media-savvy members" of the crowd speculate about whether the climber is part of a PR stunt, but then there was "counterspeculation in the crowd that the whole thing was maybe designed to maybe only *look* like a media stunt." The climber stops just below the nineteenth floor, "attached to the window and waiting."

7. SURFACE PRETENSES (PP. 42-50)

This sequence deals with the tension created by opposition between "surface pretenses" and core realities. Team

Δy's putative function is to provide objective marketing data to its employers, but in reality Team Δy is "a Captured Shop: the firm occupied a contractual space between a subsidiary of Reesemeyer Shannon Belt and an outside vendor." Team Δy's "real function" was to provide R.S.B. with data that supported what R.S.B. wanted to hear "even if the actual test data turned out to be resoundingly grim or unpromising." Team Δy conducted such a variety of tests using such a variety of different methods that "it was child's play to selectively weight and rearrange the data" into "a cascade of random noise meant to so befuddle the firm and its Client that no one would feel anything but relief at the decision to proceed."

A consumer's individual needs are in conflict with his core herd instincts. The "successful Shadow product was one that managed . . . to resonate with both these inner drives at once." The "seminal example of this sort of multivalent pitch" Schmidt usefully provides also allows him "the small secret thrill" of "tweaking Awad again." The conflict between Schmidt's pitch to the Focus Group and the belief that his work "made no difference" has him "toying dangerously with the idea of dropping the whole involved farce and simply telling the truth." The conflict between Schmidt's desire for Lilly and the impossibility of his attaining her manifests itself in his dreams and in his belief that he had "come very very close indeed to confronting" her detractors in Technical Processing.

Schmidt's inner turmoil derives from the devolution of his childhood determination (inspired by admiration for his father) "to make a difference in the affairs of men someday" into his current belief that he is "neither special nor exempt." As an employee of a Captured Shop, his only hope for advancement is a move into a job that included making surveys "that any tenth-grader could have conducted appear sophisticated and meaningful." "[E]veryone in the whole blind grinding mechanism conspired to convince each other that they could figure out how to give the paying customer what they could prove he could be persuaded to believe he wanted, without anybody once ever . . . pointing out the absurdity of calling what they were doing collecting information or even saying aloud . . . [t]hat it made no difference." "Terry Schmidt had very nearly nothing left anymore of the delusion that he differed from the great herd of the common run of men." His smile "always looked pained no matter how real the cheer," and he suffered "exaggerated bonhomie" from longtime coworkers "designed to obscure" the fact that they "had trouble recalling his name."

8. Adequately captured (pp. 50-58)

In the story's penultimate section, Schmidt informs the Focus Group members that although Team Δy would prefer to receive only one GRDS, the members may fill out as many GRDSs as necessary to insure that "their own individual feelings and preferences" are "adequately captured" (Schmidt only has 13 GRDSs though; presumably if 14 were allowed, the information might turn out to be 100% identical to the IRPs). This section features several examples of impulses being tamed or adequately captured. *Devils!* is softened to *Felonies!*, "designed to offend absolutely no one." There are detailed descriptions of the capture of two different poisons, the potential effectiveness of which is tamed by problems of administration or a narrow window of ingestion post-injection (this seems to be a good place to wonder what Schmidt's valise on p. 51 might have adequately captured). The climber successfully captures the attention of the group below, whose concern is soon replaced by "loud cries of recognition and an almost childlike delight." Schmidt's selection for his current task was in part due to his "reputation for relative conciseness and smooth preemption of digressive questions." Any surprises from the *in camera* GDRS caucuses will be adequately captured on camera.

The first-person narrator makes another overt appearance in a footnote on p. 57 to explain his intentions with respect to his emetic prosthesis, but the reasons for his mission remain elusive. He says, "We were all of us anxious to get down to business already." To whom does "all of us" refer? The narrator's "scope's Mission Time said 24:31 and change." Note that the climber began "just before 11:00 AM" (p. 13) and that some of the Focus Group members are expected to experience a sharp drop in blood sugar levels "by 11:30" (p. 18). The narrator refers to the "C.P.D.'s transmitter's clear earpiece." Wallace is meticulous about the use of periods in abbreviations; and in this story, names of advertising firms and organizations like the Chicago Fire Department (C.F.D., p. 41) are abbreviated with periods, whereas job titles like Creative Packaging Director (CPD, p. 50) are not. Therefore, the transmitter reference seems to imply that the first-person narrator either is transmitting signals to the C.P.D. (presumably the Chicago Police Department, who are indeed below with the crowd on p. 53) or is using a transmitter obtained from the C.P.D.

The idea of Mister Squishy continues to resonate throughout the story. Schmidt, who refers to himself as Mister Squishy in the mirror, uses an elaborate "squishing process" to extract poisonous ricin. Concerning the use of "squishy" as a metaphor for indecisiveness or weakness, Schmidt is unable "to enforce his preferences even in fantasy." The inflated climber is presumably meant to represent the Mister Squishy icon. "Team Δy chief Alan Britton" is "immense and physically imposing" like the inflated climber, but unlike Schmidt, he is a symbol of strength and wears "the invulnerably cheerful expression of a man who had made a difference in all he'd ever tried."

Greg Carlisle

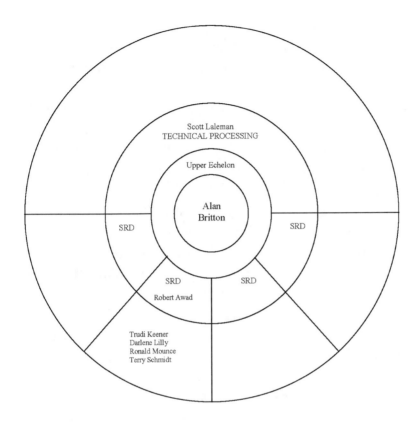

Figure 1. Team Δy Organizational Chart

9. Everything encoded (pp. 58-66)

Just as the brief street interlude on p. 5 sets up a subsequent nineteen-floor climb, the brief Britton interlude on p. 56 sets up a narrative climb to the top of the Team Δy corporate ladder (see Figure 1) in the story's final section. Wallace intensifies the narrative by shifting its central foci from Schmidt and the climber to the Team Δy hierarchy, by introducing more secret machinations, by presenting the text in one long paragraph, and by truncating the narrative before its climactic events occur; but Wallace still manages to give the reader a sense of resolution, revealing the true nature of the nested test and thereby unifying the narrative threads of the climber and the first-person narrator and the GRDS testing phase and Schmidt's concern about making a difference.

Ronald Mounce "is Robert Awad's personal mentee and probable heir apparent and is also his mole among the Field Researchers." Mounce "has been told privately" by Awad that the "Full- and No-Access Mister Squishy TFG design is in fact part of a larger field experiment that Alan Britton and Team Δy's upper management's secret inner executive circle" (incorporated by Britton as a Personal Holding Company under a dummy name) is conducting. The experiment is "designed to appeal to urban or younger consumers' self-imagined savvy about marketing tactics and 'objective' data and to flatter their sense that . . . they were . . . well nigh impossible to manipulate": to manipulate the unmanipulable. Awad's description of "the proposed campaign's Story" in which "Mister Squishy's advertisers . . . force Team Δy to manipulate and cajole Focus Groups into producing just the sort of quote unquote 'objective' statistical data needed to . . . get *Felonies!* on the shelves" seems to describe bluntly what Schmidt is doing subtly.

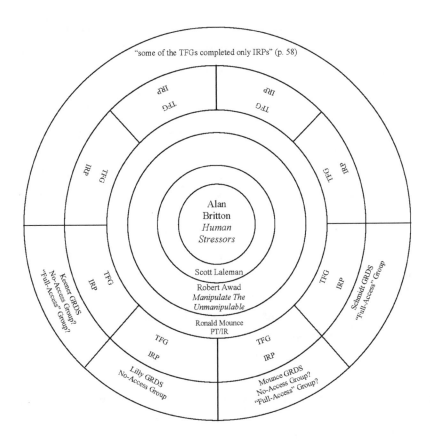

Figure 2. Team Δy Nested Tests

But as we move into Britton's sphere (see Figure 2), we learn that this is not the true nature of the test, that Britton has not incorporated a Personal Holding Company with a dummy name, and that Awad's harassment of Lilly was done as a test at Britton's instigation. (The philosophy of using testing strategies that are "extremely manipulative or abusive in the name of data" (p. 18) apparently applies to trusted employees as well as to unknown Focus Group members.) Given that "the presence of an observer affects any process," Britton (in response to R.S.B.'s Ted Belt) is attempting "to eliminate all unnecessary random variables" by "doing away as much as possible with the human element" of testing; i.e., with facilitators like Schmidt. With the use of tracking algorithms (Cookies), "the unnecessary variable of consumers even *knowing* they were part of any sort of market test was excised." The "market becomes its own test. Terrain = Map. Everything encoded," captured, tamed. All that was needed to eliminate the facilitators "was some hard study data showing unequivocally that human facilitators made a difference . . . ; they knew the numbers didn't lie; if they saw that the data entailed their own subtraction they'd go quietly." Britton intends to introduce "stressors. Nested, high-impact stimuli" into the testing environment to see "how the facilitators reacted to unplanned stimuli, how they responded to their Focus Groups' own reactions." The "sub rosa experiments' stressors would, as always in nature and hard science, determine survival." (The degree to which stressors will skew the Focus Groups' responses does not appear to be a concern.)

Britton's mentee Laleman is responsible for two Cookies being "nested deep within Team Δy's . . . protocols," a betrayal of which Britton is aware, prompting Britton to test Laleman with the stressor of impressing Britton by coming up with stressors for the experimental Focus Groups. But as Britton points a finger that "had something dark's remains in the rim around its nail," Laleman just sits there "smiling at it, his mind a great flat blank white screen." Laleman, head of Technical Processing, is unable to brainstorm, to create, to risk, to exhibit the human element. He, like Schmidt, has sacrificed experience and surprise and trust for data. Schmidt has "an apparent inability to enforce his preferences even in fantasy" (p. 55); Laleman howls upward "at what lay outside the fantasy's frame but was probably the moon." Schmidt despairs that he makes no difference; Laleman believes he has "a very special and above-average destiny." Both Schmidt and Laleman are stuck

Greg Carlisle

between conflicting desires of individualism and group membership, fated like Mounce's extinguished cigarette to "bob forever instead of sinking" or rising.

Presumably, the climber (now just below the 19th floor window) and the UAF with emetic prosthesis (the first-person narrator) will introduce stressors (presumably simultaneously) into the GRDS caucuses. How will the facilitators respond? If data can establish that Schmidt has made a difference in his Focus Group's response (and data apparently can be made to establish anything), he will lose his job by doing the very thing he desperately wants to do: make a difference. Human beings do make a difference; the nature of Britton's stressors practically guarantees a difference-making response. What is unsettling is that Schmidt might not make a difference. We, like Schmidt, are so caught between conflicting desires that we can only fantasize about and "come very very close indeed" (p. 50) to taking action. Can we still make a difference? We can't know until an opportunity arises for us to make a difference. We fear that we won't, and this is why Wallace must end the story before the stressors occur. How Schmidt will react, how we would react, remains undefined.

"Mister Squishy" seems somewhat bleak until we recall what Wallace told Larry McCaffery in the seminal 1993 interview for the Review of Contemporary Fiction: "If you operate, which most of us do, from the premise that there are things about the contemporary U.S. that make it distinctively hard to be a real human being, then maybe half of fiction's job is to dramatize what it is that makes it tough. The other half is to dramatize the fact that we still *are* human beings, now. Or can be" (McCaffery 26). "Mister Squishy" dramatizes what makes it tough to be a human being: the tension between conflicting but equal desires for group membership and individual autonomy:

between the safety and comfort of the herd and the desire to stand out, to have individual meaning, to make a difference. Group membership involves a degree of anonymity and anxiety about not making a difference, being reduced to a statistic; individual autonomy involves a degree of isolation and anxiety about forging into the unknown, making difficult choices. We cover this tension with distractions, with indecision, with satiated comfort, with fantasy, with secret manipulations, with (nested) tests to ward off surprise, with abstracted data, with oblivion. We embrace systems of marketing and advertising that prey upon our fears. Rather than working through the choices, risks, fears, and compromises that go along with establishing a taut balance between equal and contrasting desires (as in true marriage, for example); we become squishy, limbic, oblivious. Acknowledging the condition of oblivion created by our conflicting desires for individualism and group membership is a first step toward navigating our way out of oblivion's cage of stasis and realizing that "we still *are* human beings, now. Or can be." But the next steps require empathy and the risk of human contact. Isolation breeds obsession, self-indulgence, and the belief that poison can make a difference.

For readers of "Mr. Squishy," as for readers of *Infinite Jest*, the concerns of human loneliness and obsession and indecision can get lost in the extraordinary sweep of Wallace's novel inventions—inflated climbers and emetic-wearing narrators and poison plots, wheelchair assassins and magic drugs and lethal entertainments. Wallace's texts serve as analogues to the way these concerns can get lost in the various novelties we encounter in our own lives. Ken Erdedy, a marijuana addict who at one time had an advertising job, is one of the less extreme of the three-hundred-plus obsessed characters that draw our attention in *Infinite Jest*, a 1079-page novel. In Wallace's 64-page story, we are able to focus much

Greg Carlisle

more of our attention on another obsessed everyman, Terry Schmidt, who like Erdedy is driven to despair by conflicting desires. Wallace' is using the crucible of the short-story form to isolate the nature of the disease he began to identify and articulate in *Infinite Jest*. What he discovers in *Oblivion* helps him in his work on *The Pale King*, in which some of his characters are able to find a way out of their oblivion before being driven, like Erdedy and Schmidt, to desperation and dark fantasy.

"Mr. Squishy" features so many of Wallace's signature narrative techniques that his use of a pseudonym when the story was first published in McSweeney's was seen through by just about anyone even slightly familiar with his work. In addition to his undefined-climax technique (cf. Carlisle, SR 33-37), we see phrases that have to be repeated to orient the reader after a lengthy em-dash tangent (the em-dash tangent on p. 55 could have been avoided by the removal of the first phrase and the em-dashes, but Wallace uses it to call attention to contrived length in a passage about contrived length), brackets inside quotes when one character presents the speech of another character in a new context (as happens further down on p. 55), and incredibly specific detail that stands out like a fingerprint in the dust of our reading to identify a character. In documenting the lab results of Schmidt's potential poisons, Wallace uses data to mark a specific personality, whereas data is to the story's characters a means of equalizing individual personalities. The subtle shift of focus at the end of the story to new perspectives (those of Awad, Laleman, and Britton) is an evolution of the abrupt shift in perspective at the end of Wallace's early story "Solomon Silverfish."

Many of the images or motifs Wallace used in *Infinite Jest* appear here, too, including the injection of toxins into food (*IJ* 1015). The childlike Mr. Squishy icon recalls the infantile Mr. Bouncety-Bounce. The eccentric UAF's high-maintenance disguise recalls Steeply's field personas. Product testing's "cascade of random noise" recalls Marathe's "confusion of choices" (*IJ* 752). In addition to self-concerned characters with a tendency to isolate themselves and an unidentified but highly empathic narrator, "Mr. Squishy" shares with *Infinite Jest* the use of "fluorescent" (p. 3) as a pejorative adjective, humming machinery (p. 17), an attention to angles of sunlight (pp. 15, 40), cries for (or an aversion to cries for) help (p. 19), the phrase "and but so" (p. 30), potential bird omens (p. 41), an instance of a father's significant influence (p. 42), and the blurring of the terrain with the map (p. 64). A variant of the opening anecdote of *This Is Water* was featured in *Infinite Jest* (*IJ* 445), and the perception of our being at the exact center of all we experience appears here in "Mr. Squishy" too (p. 30). But the philosophy of *This Is Water* must wait for *The Pale King* to reach full bloom in Wallace's fiction.

Greg Carlisle

The Soul Is Not a Smithy

In the next-to-last sentence of Joyce's *A Portrait of the Artist as a Young Man*, Stephen Dedalus, preparing for a journey "away from home and friends," writes in his journal, "I go to encounter for the millionth time the reality of experience and to forge in the smithy of my soul the uncreated conscience of my race." This implies that our souls are furnaces where we actively heat and shape the metal of our experiences into the swords we will use as conscious agents, masters of our destinies. Wallace's title suggests that a smithy is not an accurate metaphor for the soul, given that we cannot control—and sometimes are not even consciously aware of—the way our experiences shape our personalities. Far from being conscious forgers of our destinies, we cannot know to what degree particular experiences will affect our future thoughts and actions. And no matter how much we may want to exile certain experiences into the oblivion of unconsciousness, those experiences will find a way to surface.

I. In which a traumatic incident, occurring long ago in the narrator's 4ᵗʜ grade Civics classroom, is established as the focal point of his narrative (pp. 67-69)

Wallace often uses headings to divide his work, and does so here to divide "The Soul Is Not a Smithy" into ten sections. The headings usually seem only peripherally related to the content of the section itself, and the text includes several dramatic moments that may not seem "directly relevant to the story"; but closer inspection reveals more affinity. Terence Velan, the subject of this first heading, is only discussed near the end of the section as one of several of the narrator's classmates who would transfer out of their school after a traumatic incident they experienced in their 4th grade Civics classroom at R. B. Hayes Primary School in Columbus OH on March 14, 1960. However, the information that Velan "WOULD LATER BE DECORATED IN COMBAT" serves to underscore the distance between the present narration and the traumatic event, as does "A very long time ago now" in the second paragraph and "Only much later would I understand" in the last paragraph of the section. The story is as much about the effect on the students' "subsequent lives and careers as adults later on" as it is about the traumatic incident. Several students eventually see combat duty, and indeed the story's final image is of 4th-graders charging "the papier mache bulwarks of Iwo Jima" (p. 113).

A "DRAMATIC AND FLATTERING STORY" about Velan appeared in the local paper, but his "WHEREABOUTS" upon returning home "WERE NEVER ESTABLISHED BY ANYONE MIRANDA OR I EVER KNEW OF." In the first paragraph of the section, we learn that the same local paper, writing about the traumatic incident, designated the narrator and three other "slow or problem pupils" as the "*4 Unwitting Hostages*" who created "the *hostage circumstance* that justified the taking of life" by not fleeing the classroom with the other children. Italics are used for the two phrases above, and for words like *long suffering* (p. 74) and *shellshocked* (p. 85) later, to highlight words and phrases chosen by people other than the narrator and therefore questionable or of special interest from the narrator's perspective. As usual, Wallace peppers the narrative throughout with potential mysteries and a general sense of uncertainty. Who is the "MIRANDA" of the heading? What is meant by "As with the case of my father" at the end of the section? Although many of these questions are answered as

Greg Carlisle

the story progresses, the answers to some questions, like Velan's whereabouts and the exact motivation of Mr. Johnson's actions, can never be established. Also, factual certainty is often undercut by the narrator, who describes events in great detail but frequently calls attention to potential inaccuracies, using phrases like "I can remember" (p. 68) and "this is my memory of the period" (p. 72).

2. IN WHICH THE CLASSROOM WINDOW IS ESTABLISHED AS A CANVAS UPON WHICH THE NARRATOR PROJECTS CONSTRUCTED NARRATIVE FANTASIES (PP. 70-72)

The time period during which the traumatic incident occurred was not "a time of lax discipline or disorder" (p. 69), and the narrator's classroom is obsessively ordered. Portraits of presidents are "evenly spaced around all four walls"; "bolted desks and chairs . . . were alphabetically arrayed in six rows of five pupils each"; wire mesh divided the windows on the east wall into "84 small squares with an additional row of 12 slender rectangles," upon which "discretely organized narrative fantasies" were constructed by the narrator. The last section of the story adds to the ordered classroom picture by describing ceiling tiles "numbering 96 total plus 12 fractional tiles at the south end" and a checkerboard floor pattern (p. 111).

The narrator has been characterized by his teachers and his parents as a daydreamer, but his "intense preoccupation" with his "imagined constructions" was "difficult and concentrated work." It's not that he lacked the ability to pay attention; it's just that his attention was "directed peripherally." Similarly, he could not comprehend the meaning of what he read but could remember a wealth of "specific quantitative information" about the text. Mysteriously, this reading problem went away shortly after the traumatic incident.

Wallace gives us specific information about who sits where in the alphabetical array, seemingly inviting us to track this data for its potential significance. Ahearn and Barr are in the first two of five seats in row one by the west wall; the latter Swearingen twin is in the first seat of the sixth row by the east wall; and the narrator is "in the second to last desk in the easternmost row." Blemm, Caldwell, and DeMatteis presumably complete the first row, while Velan sits somewhere in the sixth.

Perhaps the biggest mystery involves determining to what degree the narrator's real life experiences influence his imagined constructions and the relative significance of that determination. Previous constructions in the classroom window "for much of Mr. Johnson's three weeks" (the narrator normally sits near the wall opposite the windows, but the students, prompted by the introduction of a substitute teacher, have reversed the seating chart for their amusement) have featured his "terrified older brother and his piano teacher" and "a markedly familiar looking Robin."

3. IN WHICH IT MAY BE INFERRED THAT EXTREME MOODS AND COMPULSIVE BEHAVIORS ARE NOT NECESSARILY THE RESULT OF MENTAL DISTURBANCE OR CRIMINAL IMPULSE, BUT RATHER ARE INEXPLICABLE OR PERHAPS MANIFEST AS THE DESPERATE RELIEF OF LONG SUFFERING (PP. 73-74)

After the heading's announcement that Mr. Johnson, the substitute teacher who instigates the traumatic incident, "WAS LATER REVEALED TO HAVE NO RECORD OF MENTAL DISTURBANCE OR CRIMINAL BEHAVIOR," the text of the third section does not mention Mr. Johnson further, mirroring the behavior of the narrator who will be too busy constructing narrative fantasies in the window to be aware of the traumatic incident until it is well under way. The section primarily concerns two dogs that appear through the window

Greg Carlisle

on the day of the incident, prompting the narrator's memory of his brother's account (the narrator "would have been too young to remember") of the disappearance of the family dog immediately after the dog ruined an antique piano and his brother's threat of violence (note reference to "difficulties" that "began to emerge" in the narrator's brother's early adolescence) if the narrator ever brought up the incident to their mother. The black dog with a dun chest mounts the brindle-colored dog, either to mate or just to assert dominance, his expression the same "as on a human being's face when he is doing something that he feels compulsively driven to do and yet does not understand just why he wants to do it." Attempting to characterize the brindle-colored dog's expression, the narrator recalls how his mother characterized the expression of his Aunt Tina, who "had profound physical problems," as *long suffering*. The dogs will serve as the trigger for the narrator's imaginative constructions in the window until the actions of Mr. Johnson and the classroom command all of his attention.

4. IN WHICH DOGS FEATURE PROMINENTLY IN TALES OF DISTURBED FAMILIES (PP. 75-80)

The next heading appears to digress by introducing new classmates Unterbrunner, Oehmke, and Llewellyn. (The section also introduces Kone. Note that the narrator's last name must begin with a "U" or "V" given that Unterbrunner is "[d]irectly ahead" of him and therefore Velan must be behind him.) The story about Mandy Blemm's "DISTURBED FAMILY" and their dog also appears to be peripheral at first. But the previous section described the narrator's possibly disturbed family and their "disappeared" dog, and in this section the narrator constructs a narrative about a disturbed family and their missing dog. (A dog, S. Johnson, also features prominently in the tale of one of *Infinite Jest*'s disturbed families, the Incandenzas.)

The narrator continues to call attention to the subjective nature of his memory: "I do not recall," "do not remember," "[t]o the best of my recollection," "in my memory," and "before I was old enough to remember anything" all appear on p. 76. And the narrator says of his constructions in the window's mesh that he does not "hold each square's illustrated tableau in memory." But Wallace pointedly reminds his readers of significant facts or events they should keep in their memories. The narrator wonders whether Mr. Johnson was "survived by a wife," which reminds us that Mr. Johnson will die. The narrator mentions his family's antique table again and later says that the dog in his story "never chews on anything," suggesting that the disappearance of the family dog in his (supposedly unaware and unremembered) youth had such an impact that when he sees dogs in his 4th grade classroom window his thoughts return to that event. We are reminded that the story of the 4th grade trauma of March 1960 is being told from a future vantage point by the fact that Unterbrunner "would later become an administrative secretary" and by reference to young girls listening to the Everly Brothers. We are reminded "that the mental work of what [teachers and administration] called daydreaming often required more effort and concentration that it would have taken simply to listen in class." Mention is made of the narrator's father's "nerves" and how his brother "eventually turned out," continuing to fuel the impression that the narrator's family is possibly disturbed.

In fact, right after mentioning his father and brother, the narrator dives right into his constructed narrative, perhaps to avoid thinking of them further, which mirrors what he did that day in March 1960 to avoid noticing what Mr. Johnson was doing in the classroom. The constructed narrative about Ruth

Greg Carlisle

Simmons and her family features the two dogs the narrator was actually seeing outside the window that day—a "brindle-colored" dog (imagined to be Ruth's dog, Cuffie) and a "black and dun" dog—plus the imaginative addition of a "predominately piebald" dog. We are pointedly reminded in this constructed narrative of Ruth's blindness, of the wealth of her father's employer, and of her mother's tendency to seek a state of semiconsciousness.

5. In which various attempts at oblivion are unsuccessful (pp. 80-85)

In the most succinct of the story's ten headings, the narrator states that he "HAD NO IDEA WHAT WAS GOING ON," a description applicable to both the narrator and Mr. Johnson with respect to Mr. Johnson's behavior, to Ruth Simmons in the constructed narrative, to Dr. Biron-Maint's interpretation of the incident, and perhaps most significantly to the narrator's ignorance of the degree to which the unfolding incident from his childhood would continue to affect his life. In this section, attempts to suppress undesirable thoughts and actions do not meet with much success. The present-day narrator jumps to the day after the incident only to land on an image of blood, then retreats to his constructed narrative of that day, and finally returns to a post-incident image of Dr. Biron-Maint, who "gave many of us the willies even more than Mr. Johnson." Reality encroaches on the narrator's constructed fiction as well: it features a "burled walnut" table like the one that resulted in the disappearance of his dog (cf. pp. 76, 81), a "long suffering" father, Ruth Simmons's face "tilted upwards" like Mr. Johnson's (cf. pp. 76, 82), a reference to his uncle's war wound, and the removal of snow on a driveway "like a chalkboard being cleaned." Mr. Johnson's troubles surface in the words he is compelled to write on the chalkboard. Dr. Biron-Maint's diagnosis, "*shellshocked*," is labeled "crude and erroneous" by the narrator, implying that the true nature of the trauma is far more complex. Although the children are "still in shock" (p. 81) the next day, their shock is not solely or even primarily a result of shells successfully fired at Mr. Johnson but rather is a reaction to the nature and unexplained cause of Mr. Johnson's intensely troubled behavior: to the fact that no one, including Mr. Johnson, had any idea what was going on.

6. IN WHICH THE CLASSROOM ENVIRONMENT DURING THE EARLY STAGES OF THE TRAUMATIC INCIDENT IS DESCRIBED, WITH PARTICULAR EMPHASIS ON THE (IN)ATTENTIVENESS OF THE SO-CALLED 4 UNWITTING HOSTAGES (PP. 85-88)

In the 4th grade, Chris DeMatteis "COULD NOT STAY AWAKE IN HIS CLASSES" because he had to get up early to help his father. Mandy Blemm "never paid attention or completed any of her assignments" except under threat of transfer to another school like former classmate Tim Applewhite. On the day of the incident, Frankie Caldwell "had his head down and was drawing something." The narrator continued to construct his narrative, but was also aware of the total number of words on the chalkboard and of statistical facts about those words, which "were simply part of the whole peripheral environment," "there regardless of whether you're paying attention" or not. Although the narrator is remembering the details of that day's constructed narrative in his report to us years later, he says it was rare to carry a constructed narrative over to the next day "as it was difficult to hold all the unfolding details in mind for that long." Clearly the events in the classroom and in the constructed narrative are mutually influencing each other in the narrator's mind, given that Mr. Johnson's head is "cocked curiously over to the side, not unlike a dog's" and that the narrative was becoming uncharacteristically "gruesome" and "unpleasant."

Wallace tests our attentiveness and ability to hold information by giving us more student names to place in our seating chart: Ellen Morrison and Alison Standish, the latter of whom was absent the day of the incident. Tim Applewhite was presumably transferred in 3rd grade and therefore not to be listed on our seating chart. Wallace also reminds us several times in this section that we are unable to know our futures from our present vantage point. Applewhite couldn't know he would be transferred in 3rd grade. Standish couldn't know she would later move away. DeMatteis, Caldwell, and the narrator couldn't know on the day of the incident what their future jobs (identified by the narrator in this section) would be.

7. IN WHICH THE NARRATOR SUGGESTS "THAT THE MOST VIVID AND ENDURING OCCURRENCES IN OUR LIVES ARE OFTEN THOSE THAT OCCUR AT THE PERIPHERY OF OUR AWARENESS" AND THAT "INSIGHT" INTO THESE OCCURRENCES OFTEN DOES NOT HAPPEN UNTIL "MANY YEARS AFTER" (PP. 89-99)

When faced with situations that we cannot understand or resolve or that we perceive to be potentially threatening or horrible, we often buffer our discomfort or despair with an increased attention to peripheral detail or by redirecting our attention entirely in an attempt to put off dealing with those situations. These tactics are exhibited by Wallace's characters and mirrored in Wallace's text. Reality continually resists these delay tactics, though, and must eventually be countenanced with our full awareness lest we end up like Mr. Johnson, oblivious and at the mercy of his uncontrollable impulses, or like the narrator's father, burying our despair under a life of monotony.

The narrator alludes to his father's backstory in the heading, but then delays the telling until a later section. After one sentence discussing Mr. Johnson, the narrator redirects his attention and picks up his constructed narrative as Mr. Simmons's employer's "gas-powered Snow Boy device . . . stalled." In the space of that ellipsis, Wallace inserts seven lines of vivid description that evoke the operation of the device before abruptly stalling that description with the single word "stalled." The narrator's comparison of the Snow Boy device to a modified power lawnmower redirects his attention to a memory of his neighbor Mr. Snead, but this redirection does not quell the sense of classroom danger intuited by the narrator, whose constructed narrative and recounted memories continue to be infused with hints of horror and despair, influenced by the potential threat to the narrator's environment. He remembers that the lawnmower "could slice a man's hand off before he even knew what was happening" (foreshadowing the inevitable with respect to Mr. Simmons and resonant with Mr. Johnson's "not seeming to realize what he was doing"), and his memory of the Sneads quickly turns sad. Instead of going back to Mr. Simmons, he returns to one of the dogs of his constructed narrative, but the nature of the dog's backstory is so cruel and unsettling that it is "cut off abruptly." Forced to return to Mr. Simmons, the inevitable severing of limb occurs, so horrible that it shocks the narrator, who becomes "distanced enough" from his constructed narrative to become aware again "on some level" of the events in the classroom. The narrator's tactics in this sequence resonate with Wallace's, who throughout his oeuvre amasses a wealth of narrative detail leading to a crisis event, but then truncates the sequence before reaching the event to move to a new section or story.

Although aware now "on some level" of potential danger in the classroom, the narrator must still rely on what "most

Greg Carlisle

credible witnesses seemed to recall" about "the classroom's resultant confusion and fear" (as narrative attention to the classroom expands, Wallace has the narrator give us several new student names to add to our seating chart), given that he "was not conscious or attentive to any of [it] directly." He also "was not conscious of hearing" the strange sounds made by Mr. Johnson. Now "in retrospect," however, the narrator admits of the classroom's subconscious influence on the events of his constructed narrative, prompting him to leave the thread of the traumatic incident to return to those events, "which required tremendous energy and concentration to sustain."

The narrator returns to Ruth Simmons in her classroom, but the blind and deaf students are cruel to her. The deaf students trigger a memory of a deaf boy who lived on the narrator's street, but that leads to a memory of the boy's home catching fire and his family's subsequent move even though insurance covered expenses, which mirrors the post-traumatic-incident moves of several of the narrator's 4th grade classmates. Soon the narrator leaves the cruelty of Ruth's classmates to check on Marge Simmons, but she has died in her car; the snow clogging her exhaust pipe analogous to the snow-clogged device that led to her husband's trauma, and the "distant sounds" of sirens analogous to the sounds Mr. Johnson is making. So on pages 93-94, the narrator returns to the culvert where we last saw the Simmons' lost dog, who now narrowly escapes the fate of the piebald dog with the sore that the narrator did not "initially recall" (p. 90). The image of the piebald dog's demise "was so traumatic that this narrative line was immediately stopped and replaced with a neutral view of the pipe's exterior."

This prompts the narrator's assertion that a "peripheral flash of something contextless and awful" "stayed with you the most vividly and kept popping into your mind's eye" and that "the most persistent memories of early childhood consist of these flashes." He recounts "peripheral tableaux" that feature his father, his mother, and the "far-off sound" of his brother's cries and then launches a two-and-a-half page digression (another delay tactic) on a "soundless" dream sequence from *The Exorcist* which features a "brief flash" of Father Karras's face as "the face of evil." (This film imagery was perhaps triggered by the horrific image of Marge Simmons's smeared lipstick on page 93, which recalls the memorable image of Diane Ladd's character's smeared lipstick in *Wild at Heart*, directed by David Lynch, subject of a seminal Wallace essay.) The death of Father Karras's mother is a blow to his belief that a person in his vocation "could make some kind of difference [cf. Terry Schmidt in "Mr. Squishy"] and help alleviate suffering and human loneliness, which . . . he has blatantly failed to do with his own mother," a failure that brings to mind Stephen Dedalus, who inspired this story's title.

The narrator asserts that "the most vivid and enduring occurrences of our lives are often those that occur at the periphery of our awareness" and cites the significance of that assertion to his story. He states that we "often can remember the details and subjective associations far more vividly than the event itself" (true enough given his story so far) and that often "the most vividly felt and remembered elements will appear at best tangential to someone else." After two brief images associated with the classroom that day and with his father, the narrator takes one last diversionary trip through his constructed narrative, all four threads stalled in Wallace's signature state of "Chaotic Stasis" (*IJ* 996n61). The last image of the Simmons' "defenseless, long suffering" dog being mounted by the other dog resolves into the mirror-image of the dogs "in the actual field through the classroom window" that initiated the constructed narrative back on p. 73. Like the dog, the narrator (one of four students who will not leave the classroom) decides "to sit still and endure it or else something really terrible would happen." His constructed narrative abandoned and his attention back in the classroom, the narrator can now complete his tale of the specific traumatic event of that day and reveal the equally troubling insights into his father's despair foreshadowed in this section's heading before returning to his classroom for some final thoughts.

8. In which "THE ONLY REAL TRUTH" is fear (PP. 99-102)

The narrator's recounting of the traumatic event reinforces Wallace's key themes for this story: the idiosyncrasies of memory and attentiveness, the insight of reflection on past events, and the fear of the unexplainable. The "final frame" the narrator remembers from his constructed narrative is "a close-up, stop-action view" of Ruth Simmons's clay statuette in midair, revealing it to be a human being that "she had given four legs instead of two." The narrator says, "The import of this detail in the narrative I do not remember, though I recall the detail itself very clearly." Perhaps the transition of the narrator's attention from the dogs in the window to the human beings in the classroom has influenced the shape of Ruth's statuette, which is about to be hit with a cane, just as Mr. Johnson is about to be hit with bullets.

The narrator's continual qualifications of his recounting of the traumatic event with reference to his memory makes his statement about Mr. Johnson's "indescribable" face on p. 100 stand out in sharp contrast: "I will never forget it." This was the first part the narrator "fully saw of the incident," his attention triggered by the sound of Mr. Johnson's chalk snapping and "the associated sounds and odors" of Finklepearl's vomitus. The students are "mesmerized with fear," experiencing "sheer terror." In hindsight, the narrator attributes the police's opening fire on Mr. Johnson to "MR. JOHNSON'S FACIAL EXPRESSION AND SUSTAINED HIGH SOUND, AND HIS COMPLETE OBLIVIOUSNESS TO THE OFFICER'S COMMANDS," since Mr. Johnson "HAD NOT APPEARED TO CONFRONT, RESIST, OR THREATEN THE ARMED OFFICERS." This was "ONE OF THE MOST TROUBLING AND MUCH DISCUSSED ASPECTS OF THE TRAUMA" "IN LIGHT OF THE POLITICAL SITUATION OF [THE NARRATOR'S GENERATION'S] LATER ADOLESCENCE," in which police officers harm protesters engaged in nonviolent, civil disobedience in the mid- to late-1960s. It is unclear to what degree the traumatic event influences the number of the narrator's classmates who go on to serve overseas: Caldwell and Oehmke join the list that began with Velan in the first line of the first heading of the story.

9. IN WHICH A RELATIONSHIP BETWEEN FEAR AND SILENCE IS ESTABLISHED (PP. 103-110)

The heading of this section reveals that Frankie Caldwell never corrected the press's error of classifying him as deficient or slow like the other three so-called hostages because he was deeply embarrassed about hyperventilating and losing consciousness because he was so afraid. This gets at the core truth of Wallace's story: that fear leads to silence or an avoidance of dealing with reality. In fact, the narrator is actually using the tale of the traumatic event to screen his real concern: fears about life associated with his father's job and with the uncertainties that prompt and accompany those fears. The story of the traumatic event works as an analogy to the story of his father that the narrator is actually trying to tell, because in the story of the traumatic event the narrator also attempts to displace fears by centering on other narratives while reality continues to find ways to influence his fantasy. More

Greg Carlisle

significantly analogous to the narrator's father, the essence of the traumatic event is rooted in the fear engendered by the look on Mr. Johnson's face and the inability to explain or resolve Mr. Johnson's despair, even in hindsight.

It "is in hindsight" that the narrator believes his dreams were about adult life and that he suspects "there was something of a cover-your-eyes and stop-your-ears quality to [his] lack of curiosity about just what [his] father had to do all day." But he "knew, even then, that the dreams involved [his] father's life and job and the way he looked when he returned home from work at the end of the day." During the routine of entering the foyer and removing his hat and coat, the narrator's "father's eyes appeared lightless and dead, empty." "There was something about this routine that cast shadows deep down in parts of me I could not access on my own." Of his dream the narrator says, "It was the type of nightmare whose terror is less about what you see than about the feeling you have in your lower chest about what you're seeing."

The narrator's dreams "about the reality of adult life [began] as early as perhaps age seven." Ages seven to nearly ten were the narrator's "troubling and upsetting period" (p. 72) of not being able to read, which ended within weeks of the traumatic incident in the classroom. Eventually, the dreams vanish "as abruptly as the problem with reading." The traumatic incident serves as a catalyst to eliminate the young narrator's reading problem and his dream of his father's work room; but the adult narrator still redirects attention to delay or avoid topics that involve fear and uncertainty. The narrator now discusses his visceral fantasies and dreams at an emotionally safe distance.

Describing the shift from consciousness to the oblivion of dreaming, the narrator says, "You move, gradually, from merely thinking about something to experiencing it as really there, unfolding, a story or world you are a part of, although at the same time enough of you remains awake to be able to discern on some level that what you are experiencing does not quite make sense, that you are on some cusp or edge of true dreaming." This resonates with the narrator's experience looking at his classroom window. Also, the "dream was of a large room full of men in suits and ties seated at rows of great grey desks" "arranged in precise rows and columns like the desks of an R. B. Hayes classroom."

The dream, like the dream sequence from *The Exorcist*, is terrifying in part due to its lack of sound. In contrast, the narrator's father "liked to have music or a lively radio program on and audible all of the time at home" (the sounds are like the neighborhood porch lights, "bulwarks against something without name"). The narrator's father spent his break from "the overwhelming silence he sat in all day" eating lunch on a bench in a "little square of grass and trees." In the fall the "sickly trees . . . drew swarms of migrating starlings" that "filled the mind with sound before rising again in a great mass."

Speaking of his father (and recalling the difficulties of communication discussed on p. 97), the narrator says, "I have no idea what he thought about, what his internal life might have been like[, or] what words he might have used to describe his job and the square and two trees to my mother. I knew my father well enough to know it could not have been direct." "And the idea of ever trying to tell my father about the dream was— even later, after it had vanished as abruptly as the problem with reading—unthinkable." The narrator's fear leads to silence.

"Part of the terror" of the narrator's dream "was that the men in the room appeared as both individuals and a great anonymous mass" (cf. "Mr. Squishy"). Also, for the narrator these "colorless, empty-eyed, long suffering faces were the face of some death that awaited me long before I stopped walking

Greg Carlisle

around. Then, when real sleep descended . . . the lens of perspective pulls suddenly back, and I am one of them." At some point the narrator in the dream looks "up and into the lens of the dream's perspective," and staring back at himself, "it is impossible to know what the adult me is seeing or how I am reacting or if there is anything in there at all."

10. In which details are recounted and reconsidered and meanings are "ANYONE'S GUESS" (pp. 110-113)

We learn in the final heading that the narrator's brother, via court arrangement, went on to serve in the same regiment as Terence Velan, connecting the last heading to the first and foreshadowing the war imagery of the story's end. It was the narrator's brother who first got *THE 4* thinking "STILL LATER" about Mr. Johnson's "INTENDED MEANING OF THE WORD *THEM*" in his chalkboard imperatives to *KILL THEM*. (Although entirely coincidental, note that in *Infinite Jest*, italicized words in all caps signaled words placed into Gately's head that were not his own.) Perhaps the imperatives didn't refer to the students at all. It "WAS ANYONE'S GUESS," and it will remain a mystery given that Mr. Johnson "WAS HARDLY IN A POSITION TO ELABORATE."

The narrator begins this final section of text by returning to his original tactic—to delay discussing Mr. Johnson which was in turn a tactic to delay discussing his father, the narrator's numerous tactics resonant with the "multiple coats of paint" in the classroom that "smoothed and occluded" "the uneven texture of the cinderblocks underneath"—of describing his classroom, providing additional details even as he says "I have only general, impressionistic memories of Mrs. Roseman's classroom" and changes the exact "six rows of five desks each" (p. 68) to an inexact "either 30 or 32 desks" here, perhaps prompting us to take his numerous qualifications with respect to his memory of events in 1960 more seriously. We are also disoriented by two more discoveries: in the narrator's reality, the president elected after Carter will be Rhodes, not Reagan (alternate presidential history occurs in *Infinite Jest*, too); and Ruth Simmons was a classmate of the narrator's just a month before her central role in his constructed narrative. Surely the narrator would have mentioned the real Ruth Simmons if she was still in the classroom in March 1960? How resonant is the trauma in his constructed narrative with Ruth's actual reasons for leaving the class? On the other hand, could the narrator be misremembering Reagan's name to have been Rhodes and his imagined Ruth Simmons to have been an actual classmate? Constructing a classroom seating chart to help resolve the question of Ruth's status as imaginary or real proves to be quite difficult and requires a lengthy digression which begins after the next paragraph.

There is no reference to Mr. Johnson past the fifth line of each of the two paragraphs here. In fact, the reference to Mr. Johnson's holding his chalk "like a toy sword" triggers the narrator's attempt to put distance between traumatic events by retreating a month further into the past, but reality intrudes there too. And the only real truth is fear. The recounting of the February 1960 President's Day presentation features references to Ruth Simmons, the narrator's father who "got permission to leave work early," the narrator's absent mother who "was again not feeling up to par," and DeMatteis's eerie mantra of "Fear itself." And although "Oehmke and several other boys" played make-believe by charging "papier mâché bulwarks of Iwo Jima" with "broomsticks and aluminum foil bayonets," they were wearing "their fathers' helmets and tags."

Greg Carlisle

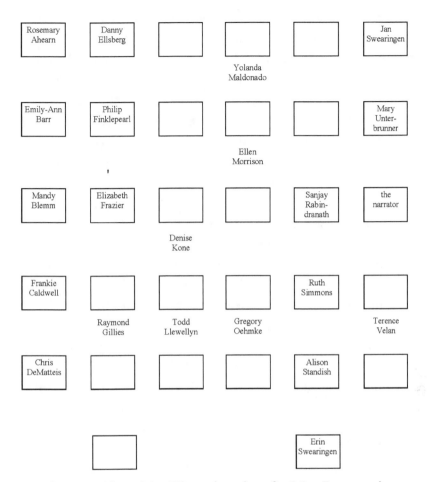

Figure 3. Altered (p. 70) seating chart for Mrs. Roseman's
4th grade Civics class, March 14, 1960

Figure 3 is an attempt to construct a seating chart based
on several assumptions, many of which are quite tenuous. It will
be helpful to consider Figure 3 as we work through these
assumptions. It is assumed that Mrs. Roseman would not alter
her alphabetical seating chart in the middle of the year when a
student withdrew from school unless incoming transfers
required an alteration. It is assumed that no students have

transferred into the 4th grade class this year. It is assumed that rows one through six refer to vertical rows of desks/students from west to east, excepting reference to a horizontal front row on p. 101. It is assumed that there are 32 desks in the classroom, not 30. To ensure an exact reversal of the seating chart for Mr. Johnson's classes (p. 70), the two extra desks would need to be in either rows one and six, two and five, or three and four. Assuming that Ruth Simmons is real and that she moved away in February or March 1960, those extra desks are assumed to be in rows two and five. Students that cannot be accurately placed in a desk are placed between desks.

Sanjay Rabindranath's position is to the narrator's "immediate left," and the "latter of the Swearingen twins [(Jan) is] at the front of the easternmost row" (p. 70); placing Erin Swearingen at the end of the fifth row with two empty desks between her and Rabindranath for former student Ruth Simmons and absent student Alison Standish (p. 87). If there are only 30 desks, there is no room for Ruth Simmons, which could mean the seating chart was rearranged in mid-year or that Ruth Simmons was never there and the narrator is merging fantasy with reality.

The fact that the narrator's position is "in the second to last desk in the easternmost row" (p. 70) to the immediate right of Rabindranath requires another assumption. In *Infinite Jest*, Wallace often uses words or phrases that allow for a range of interpretation. Does "midnight" refer to the end of one day or the beginning of the next? What is the exact age of a "toddler"? Mario *is* "eighteen in May," be he *turned* eighteen the previous November. And so on. For our seating chart to be useful, "second to last" must mean the second *from* the last desk instead of the penultimate desk: starting in the southeast corner and counting up the sixth row the series would then be last desk, next to last desk, second to last desk, etc. (But why not just say the middle desk in the easternmost row then?)

In order for our chart to work, we also must assume there is an error on p. 86: "Chris DeMatteis had his head on his desk in the [first row, not the] second row." Our assumption is justified by DeMatteis "in the rear of his row" and by "Ahearn and Ellsberg and others in the front [horizontal] row" (p. 101). The class only "started . . . rising from their desks" after DeMatteis's "panicked cry of awakening" (p. 101). Although quite a stretch, our chart shows that Frazier and Barr could conceivably be leaning over or away from their desks and "holding on to each other" as they are said to be doing on page 92 before the class "started . . . rising from their desks" on page 101. (If DeMatteis is in the second row, then Ellsberg is in the third row, in front of Finklepearl and Frazier, placing Frazier even further out of range of Barr than our chart currently places her.) It would be convenient to assume an extra desk in row one and then assume that Tim Applewhite (p. 86) was transferred after he began 4th grade, leaving the second desk empty, moving everyone else back a desk, and placing Barr and Frazier next to one another. But this would require a matching extra desk in row six instead of row five, which won't work because Sanjay Rabindranath must be to the narrator's "immediate left" (p. 70).

Structurally and thematically this story is reminiscent of *Infinite Jest*. "The Soul Is Not a Smithy" begins in the present and then uses March 1960 as a narrative focal point before slipping back to a memory of February 1960 for its conclusion. *Infinite Jest* begins in November 2010 and then uses November 2009 as a narrative focal point before slipping back to a memory of early 2002. Also, several narrative threads at the end of *Infinite Jest* close with images and ideas reminiscent of the opening of those threads. One of the major themes of *Infinite*

Jest concerns the influence of fathers on their children, and our last image of Hal finds him despairing over the endless loop of life's routine. There is a long list of other commonalities between the two works. *Infinite Jest* also uses long headings that are part of the story rather than outside it. Hal's report of the mold incident is based primarily on his brother's memory and not what he remembers. Consider also twilight sadness (pp. 80, 104), Dr. Biron-Maint's nose (pp. 81, 85) which recalls the hypophalangial grief therapist, neglectful parents (pp. 81, 96), Mr. Johnson's sustained horrific sound (pp. 91-2) which recalls the contribution of the recording of Linda McCartney's isolated and vulnerable backup singing to *Infinite Jest*'s final horror scene, images of claws (pp. 92, 93), thick glass and deep water (p. 95), the face of evil (p. 97) like the face in the floor of Hal's nightmares, that tip-of-the-tongue feeling (p. 97), infant imagery and Mr. Johnson's indescribable face (p. 100) which recalls Kevin Bain, a face pressed against glass (p. 102), the horror of fluorescence (p. 105), the fear of vacancy (p. 110) that recalls Hal's opening declaration "I am in here," and Mr. Johnson frozen and transported (p. 112) like Ken Erdedy.

Like "Mr. Squishy" and most of the stories in *Oblivion*, "The Soul Is Not a Smithy" also features nested narratives (see Figure 4). Rather than providing a hierarchy of metanarrative perspectives as in "Mr. Squishy," here the nesting puts distance between traumatic events and serves as a coping mechanism for underlying fears or effects of trauma. Dreams and fantasies served to buffer the narrator's underlying anxieties until about age 10, but upon the abrupt departure of his reading problem and of his dream of his father's work room, his defense against anxiety is increasingly fortified by memory lapses, distance from events, and intellectual rationalizations.

Greg Carlisle

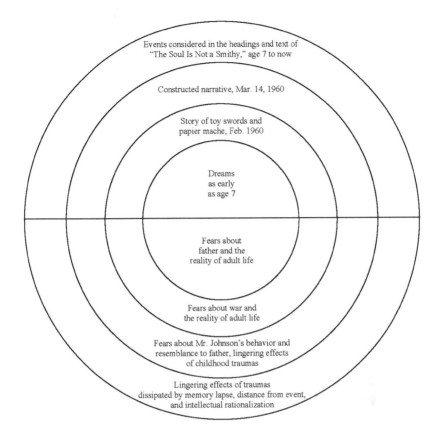

Figure 4. Nested narratives viewed as coping mechanisms for the narrator's underlying fears in "The Soul Is Not a Smithy"

The narrator of "The Soul Is Not a Smithy" comes closer than most characters in the book to balancing consciousness and oblivion. In fact, Michael Pietsch, who selected from Wallace's papers and notes the material that comprises *The Pale King*, considered inclusion of this text as a chapter in *The Pale King*. Although this text did not appear in *The Pale King*, §23 of the unfinished novel is highly resonant with the ninth section of this story (and in §32 *The Exorcist* is also significant). But although the narrator of "The Soul Is Not a Smithy" is aware of the experiences that have shaped him (especially his fear of the boredom that his father experienced) and consciously reflects upon them, his tendency to keep those experiences at bay with a wealth of narrative detail is a still a form of oblivion.

Greg Carlisle

Incarnations of Burned Children

Sounds and silences are both associated with horror in Wallace's work. In "The Soul Is Not a Smithy," nightmares are silent, and Mr. Johnson's sustained high sound is frightening. In this story, a single three-page paragraph, a child learns "to leave himself," coping with his horror by transitioning from sound to silence, to vapor. Wallace's narrative mirrors the child's experience. Across four movements, "the tenant's door" breaks away from the house as the child transitions to a "life untenanted," and the story moves from sounds made in the present to the silence of memory.

1. Separate from the sounds that issued

The story opens with the grounding image of the tenant's door being attached to the house. The Daddy leaves his work when he hears "the child's screams and the Mommy's voice gone high between them," "matching the screams with cries of her own, hysterical so she was almost frozen." The "screen door had banged shut behind him." The child seemed "somehow separate from the sounds that issued." The Daddy also copes with this horror by separating from the issuing sounds: "he'd ceased to hear the high screams because to hear them would freeze him."

2. A high pure shining sound

The door is now "half off its top hinge." A bird, often ominous in Wallace's work, is not said to sing but "to observe the door with a cocked head." Wallace often associates fluttering with terror, and here the Mommy has "one hand waving around in the area of her mouth and uttering objectless words" while the child makes "a high pure shining sound."

3. HE SCREAMED FOR THEM TO HELP HIM

The climactic movement of this short piece, a single sentence, begins with the Mommy "talking singsong at the child's face and the lark on the limb with its head to the side and the hinge going white in a line from the weight of the canted door until the first seen wisp of steam came lazy from under the wrapped towel's hem." Why did the parents overlook, why did we overlook, the "baggy diaper" in the eighth line of the story? The removal of the towel and diaper initiates the shift from sound to silence and from immediacy to distance. The Daddy "threw a haymaker at the air of the kitchen and cursed." Although the child mirrors the Daddy with "stricken motions of his hands in the air," he does not mirror the Daddy's speech and "might now have been sleeping if not for the rate of his breathing." The image of the child's hands leads to a memory of those hands clutching the Daddy's thumb while the child "watched [not heard] the Daddy's mouth move in song, his head cocked [like the bird's] and seeming to see past him into something his eyes made the Daddy lonesome for in a sideways way." The child has an early memory of his newly embodied self (a self that can still see the something-before-embodiment that the father can't see but that the father has enough of a distant intimation of to be lonely for "in a sideways way") and of the grounding security provided by his father's thumb just before the child learns to become less embodied in the wake of his father's failure to help him.

Greg Carlisle

4. So much vapor aloft

The Daddy too has a memory of a song, "as if the radio's lady was almost there with him looking down at what they've done," before the narrative leaps forward to "hours later" in order to look back (or down) at events subsequent to the removal of the diaper. But "by then it was too late, when it wouldn't stop and they couldn't make it the child had learned to leave himself and watch the whole rest from a point overhead." The child's leaving himself is a complex process tending to abstraction that Wallace makes simple and concrete for us by tracking the measured, inevitable separation of the tenant's door from the house: "half off its top hinge," "the weight of the canted door," "the hinge gave." The child "lived its life untenanted, a thing among things, its self's soul so much vapor aloft" (the vapor reminiscent of the "first seen wisp of steam"). The burned child is still incarnate, his soul is bound to his untenanted body, but from a place above, forever overhead, "falling as rain and then rising" (see Figure 5).

This story is unique for Wallace in that he describes for us a crisis event, moving linearly through rising action to a climax and denouement. Normally, details metastasize as the narrative approaches a crisis event that remains undefined.

Wallace spares us a description of what's underneath the diaper, but the crisis event of removing the diaper occurs, initiating a spike of peak tension followed by the relief of the child's releasing his soul to "a point overhead." Although the structure of the story is unique for Wallace, there are recurring motifs and images: aural horror, unsettling silence, an ominous bird, parents (one frozen between choices) who do not help a child, "eyes rolled up" in pain.

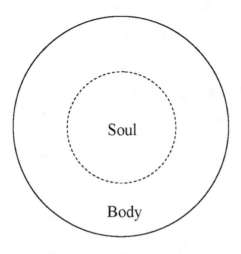

Figure 5a. Standard Incarnations

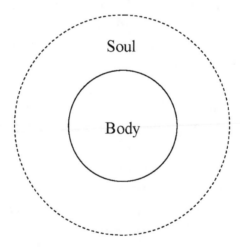

Figure 5b. Incarnations of Burned Children

Consider this passage from *Infinite Jest* that comes near the end of a biographical sketch of Mario:

People who're somehow burned at birth, withered or ablated way past anything like what might be fair, they

Greg Carlisle

either curl up in their fire, or else they rise. Withered saurian homodontic Mario floats, for Hal. He calls him Booboo but fears his opinion more than probably anybody except their Moms's. Hal remembers the unending hours of blocks and balls on the hardwood floors of early childhood . . . huge-headed Mario hanging in there for games he could not play, for make-believe in which he had no interest other than proximity to his brother. Avril remembers Mario still wanting Hal to help him with bathing and dressing at thirteen—and age when most unchallenged kids are ashamed of the very space their sound pink bodies take up—and wanting the help for Hal's sake, not his own. (*IJ* 316-7)

The first sentence of course has striking similarities to this story, although Mario was not literally burned; in fact, he is almost impervious to pain and has been burned without feeling it (*IJ* 589). But Mario is a joyful, other-oriented person, which seems unlikely for the burned child, who "lived its life untenanted, a thing among things."

So far, the characters in *Oblivion* have not achieved a better balance of consciousness and oblivion than those in *Infinite Jest*. Terry Schmidt is as keen an observer of detail as Hal, but like Hal, his thoughts agitate and isolate him. The narrator of "The Soul Is Not a Smithy" has buried his youthful traumas under protective layers of consciousness just as Don Gately has, traumas that begin to surface months after Gately's rise out of the oblivion of drug use. And although Gately is not nearly as analytical as many of Wallace's characters, it is clear that Gately has become more other-oriented and has a heroic dedication to staying substance-free that requires equal doses of non-analytical thinking and mental discipline. Gately pursues a heroic goal; it is unclear why the narrator of "The Soul Is Not a Smithy" is telling us his story. Mario is physically damaged, but present, engaged, beloved by all; the burned child seems to have completely separated his conscious being from his oblivious body, although who can blame him for this coping mechanism? But, unlike most of the characters in *Oblivion*, some characters in *The Pale King*, like IRS-workers Chris Fogle and Meredith Rand, will be able to acknowledge, articulate, and provide context for their traumas in a more direct, less obscured way.

Greg Carlisle

Another Pioneer

Like the previous story, "Another Pioneer" is a single-paragraph story about a uniquely incarnated child. Like the next story, it contains the idea that self-consciousness can lead to one's thinking of oneself as a fraud. Like "Mr. Squishy" it deals with the tension between conscious individualism and the oblivious herd. Like "The Soul Is Not a Smithy," its core narrative is distanced from its framing narrative.

1. THE ADVENT OF THIS CHILD (PP. 117-126)

"Another Pioneer" values opposing ideas equally: immediacy vs. distance, the archetypal vs. the quotidian, the primitive vs. the modern, and uncertainty vs. context/unity. The narrator privileges the immediacy of the spoken story, retelling what he "heard aloud" to a gathering of gentlemen who presumably have a common interest in a particular archetypal narrative cycle. But a sense of distance and uncertainty interrupts the immediacy and unity of the retold story: the narrator is thrice-removed from the story he is retelling (see Figure 6), a story he complicates by describing as a "variant or *exemplum*," and the primitive story is both discussed from a modern perspective (the contrast is often a source of humor) and dissected critically.

The narrator comments on the unexceptional circumstances in which the original story was told—teller and listener both "average and unremarkable" United airline passengers—and on the "even more banal and unexpected . . . quotidian . . . modern *everydayness* of the narrative circumstances" of the subsequent retelling by the narrator's friend's acquaintance to his friend. He also comments on the original telling's lack of context, the original story seeming to come from "out of nowhere." The narrator's friend's acquaintance "missed the first part of whatever larger conversation it was part of" and found it "difficult to extrapolate anything from" the airline passengers. Similarly, we join Wallace's story already in progress (the first word we read is "Nevertheless"), and we can't determine exactly why the gentlemen are gathered.

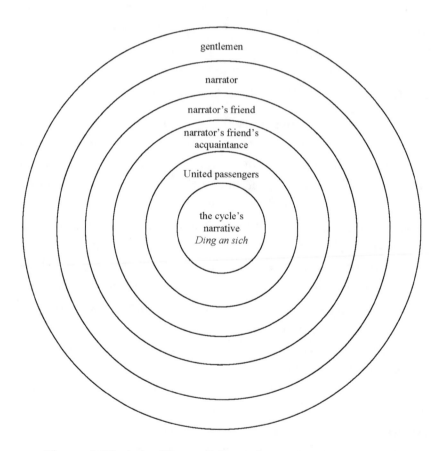

Figure 6. Nested tellings of the archetypal narrative cycle

Greg Carlisle

In what is described as the "protasis" of the core narrative, a child prodigy whose "preternatural brilliance . . . extends even to those questions that are considered by the village supremely important" is "called upon to adjudicate very complex and multifaceted conflicts" in his village. The child is deemed to have "come spontaneously into incarnated form," invested with "unique unprecedented legal status," relocated to "a special sort of raised wicker dais or platform in the precise geometric center of the village," visited "once every lunar cycle" by villagers "with questions and disputes for him to resolve via ethical *fatwa*," and compensated for those services.

In this village of hunters and gatherers, "there was evidently nothing like actual barter or trade until the advent of this child who could and would answer any question put to it." In another instance of the village's cultural evolution, "the shaman and midwife castes began to cultivate the intellectual or as it were rhetorical skill of structuring a monthly question in such a way as to receive a maximally valuable answer from the extraordinary child, and they began to sell or barter these interrogatory skills to ordinary villagers . . . , which was the advent of what the narrative apparently terms the village's *consultant caste*."

We are often reminded of the levels of mediation between the core narrative and the present retelling. The narrator often interrupts his narrative to describe and speculate on the United passengers and disclaims that he is "substituting my friend's own terminology for that of the analytical younger man on the United flight" and that "it was not clear whether my friend or his acquaintance were providing their own examples or whether these were actual examples enumerated during the dialogue he overheard on the United flight" and "that but at certain points it became unclear what was part of the cycle's narrative's *Ding an sich* and what were the passenger's own editorial interpolations and commentary."

The protasis concludes with "upper-caste citizens" from a neighboring dominant village appearing before "their tyrannical shaman" (who in contrast with the advanced child at the center of his village "evidently dwells . . . just outside the dominant village's city limits") to express their concern about the advanced child's village becoming a threat to their own village.

2. The child's psychic withdrawal (pp. 126-130)

"[W]e are told that the original *exemplum* splits or diverges here into at least three main epitatic variants." In each of the variants the advanced child "withdraws its consciousness into some type of meditative catatonic state," whether triggered by a whispered question, a spell, or the village's own inevitable sophistication. The dominant village's shaman plays an active part in the first two variants, "susurrating some question" or delivering the "mutant glyph-excrescent breadfruit" to which is affixed "some potion or spell." Resonant with the second variant, the *exemplum* as a whole—delivered by a United passenger whose "unusual patch of grey or prematurely white hair" "seemed if gazed at long enough to comprise some sort of strange intaglial glyph"—has a spellbinding quality, given its repeated tellings and the import with which the narrator explicates it to the other gentlemen. Projecting modern cultural evolution onto the primitive story, the child's "oneirically catatonic mystical state" is said to be "rather like a mainframe compiling." The narrator will make use of several more computer analogies in subsequent pages.

In the third "rather more passively modernistic epitatic variant," the shaman divines that "it will be the very questions the child is asked by the increasingly modernized and

Greg Carlisle

sophisticated villagers that will facilitate the *wunderkind*'s further development into something so supernaturally advanced that it will ultimately prove the upstart village's very undoing." In this variant "the malevolent shaman is reduced from a peripeteiac antagonist to a mere vehicle for exposition or foreshadowing." Wallace counters the expansion of the narrative into variants (which includes references to "sub- and sub-sub-versions" of variants, too) by providing a bare-bones explication of the epitatic variants in half the space he used for the protasis and will use for the catastasis. But although "the jetliner's somewhat pedantic young narrator" asserts "that the mythopoeic narrative's very structure itself moves from initial unity to epitatic trinity to reconciliation and unity again in the falling action," the narrator will continue to point out narrative alternatives influenced by the variants and sub-variants in the putatively reunified catastasis.

3. THE ADVANCED BOY'S RELATION TO AS IT WERE BOTH TRUTH AND CULTURE (PP. 130-140)

The unity of the catastasis (which the present narrator initiates with "Nevertheless," as he initiated the protasis) is challenged by its expansion and complexity as it moves through three evolving stages and "at least some of the archetypal catastrophe" while also considering variants and introducing flashbacks. (The present narrator even gets confused coming out of a flashback to the protasis: "but now in the epi—pardon me in the catastasis.") In the first stage, the post-trance child "resumes answering the cyclic queue of villagers' questions," but "he now understands his answers as part of a much larger network or system of questions and answers and further questions instead of being merely discrete self-contained units of information."

In the second stage, "the child begins the even more troubling practice of responding to a villager's question with questions of his own." In response to a villager's question about the timing of his willful daughter's clitoridectomy, the child asks, "What might one suppose to be the equivalent of a clitoridectomy for willful sons?" The advanced child, like most modern cultures, has evolved beyond barbaric, gender-exclusive practices, but "note here please" that the present narrator's audience is a gathering of "gentlemen," albeit gentlemen who presumably would not condone clitoridectomies. The child also suggests that belief in the village's Yam Gods might be a case of everyone "aping what they in turn saw everyone else behaving as if they believed" and feeling "themselves to be a secret hypocrite or fraud": another case of individual, enlightened thought introducing tension into traditional, collective thought. The child theorizes that "in the absence of any normative cultural requirement to fear and distrust the Yam Gods" a condition of mutual *agape* love between the villagers and their Gods might occur. The image of "agape" villagers four lines later calls to mind Gaddis's posthumous, single-paragraph novel, *Agape Agape*, which begins in the middle of a monologue. The narrator interrupts himself to point out that the United "passenger's articulation of the child's response [was] frequently interrupted with pedantic analytical asides and glosses." Although the child's responses send "questioners staggering back to their lean-tos to lie curled foetally on their sides with rolling eyes and high fevers as their primitive CPUs tried frantically to reconfigure themselves," the village's ritual (like its belief in its Yam Gods) had "become such an entrenched social custom that the villagers [felt] terrific unease and anxiety at the thought of abandoning it."

In the third stage, "after several more lunar cycles," the child responds to the villagers' questions by "appearing almost to berate them" for asking "dull, small, banal, quotidian, irrelevant questions" rather than "the really important questions." The consultant caste now has "nothing better to do all day than hold seminars for the angry villagers in which for some type of fee the consultants will advance and debate various theories about what exactly has happened to the child." Consultants "theorize about just what fatal question" might have been whispered to the boy "with various sub-versions' consultants arguing for every sort of possible question," of which the "untold other examples" that could have been added to the present narrator's three were obscured in the original telling by "ambient engine and cabin noise." Just as the original telling was threatening to reroute into an unresolved examination of narrative variants, there was "at least one interval during which it looked as though [the plane was] going to be rerouted and forced to land somewhere other than [its] scheduled destination."

Recalling the whispered question that (in some variants) triggers a "lethal involution" in the child that "resonates with malignant-self-consciousness themes" in archetypal narratives, it is the child's whispered answer to a village warrior's question after "the rest of the queue has dispersed" that drives the warrior "hopelessly insane." Because "Another Pioneer" is a story in part about storytelling, Wallace appropriately has the present narrator question how the "narrator on the United flight justifies including [the child's answer to the warrior] in the catastasis" (to which we might say: because it triggers the catastrophe), given that the warrior's death by "predacious jaguars" leaves the villagers with no way to link his death to his advanced-child-triggered insanity. The villagers stop making contact with the child in the hopes that he will starve to death, but the child has prepared for this turn of events. "[S]omething along the lines of" what the shaman "had in fact whispered" to the child ("in the catastasis of the first epitatic variant") is revealed in a "flashback or interpolation" that illustrates how the shaman sowed seeds of doubt that might have made the child think of himself as a fraud, gives the child the idea to hoard food, and predicts the villagers' starvation tactic that leaves the child in "his own utter isolation."

The plane descends as the story moves through its falling action, and "at least some of" the story's catastrophe—in which the villagers abandon their village and the boy at its center "to return to hunting and gathering and sleeping beneath trees"—is overheard as passengers "assemble themselves for disembarkation" (prepare to abandon their plane). The consultants "follow[ed] the herd as they had before the dawn of time." Warriors set fire to the village, at the center of which (in some variants) "the motionless boy [was] still seated," "the morning breeze spreading the blaze in a great phlogistive hiss as from a dissatisfied crowd," the blaze "a great rapacious fire that grew and gained ground no matter how hard the high castes drove them."

There are some motifs in "Another Pioneer" that resonate with those in *Infinite Jest*. Like the boy in the story, Hal is a child prodigy whose advanced intelligence, upon reaching maturity, isolates him and whose attempts at communication are met with fear. In "Another Pioneer," the older child's responses to their questions induce some villagers "to lie curled foetally on their sides" in distress. In *Infinite Jest*, drug abuse and an irresistible film induce in users/viewers an infantile and catatonic comfort, at least at first. The rapid cultural evolution of the child and his village suggests that the potential for human advancement has been possible since primitive times and that human advancement and decline is more or less the cyclical reenactment of an archetypal human

Greg Carlisle

narrative. Near the end of *Infinite Jest*, Hal feels "as if all this had been done and said so many times before it made you feel it was recorded" (*IJ* 966). The torchbearers of the "great rapacious fire" of enlightenment and its consequences are storytellers. The engine of *Infinite Jest* ignites when Hal knowingly predicts that someone will soon ask him "So yo then man what's *your* story?" (*IJ* 17)

Enlightenment in isolation leads to "malignant-self-consciousness." Our protective, herd instincts make us mistrust the change enlightened advancement requires. Stories allow us to consider acting on radical ideas without feeling threatened, because we can hear how fictional characters fare first and learn from them. Stories, especially stories "heard aloud," are shared, like a conversation. (Even what a cloistered author puts down on paper must be crafted to be understood by others. Inherent in the act of writing is an intention to share, regardless of whether the final manuscript is shared or not.) Stories shared in groups and repeated through the ages are especially powerful, ritualistic. Ideally, gatherings fend off malignant self-consciousness without devolving into the comfort of groupthink. Alternately, in *Infinite Jest*, the automatic acceptance of the trite clichés repeated ritually by the AA herd blazes a trail from oblivion to consciousness for many of its members, Gately in particular. The purpose of the gathered gentlemen of "Another Pioneer" and the nature of their group remains unclear.

A pioneer is an individual that goes first, explores new territory, paves the way for others. Inherent in the pioneering discovery, whether of new lands or new ideas, is the expectation of followers. The pioneer cannot be considered a pioneer unless the discovery is shared and passed on to other people who learn and rediscover, who tell the story of the original discovery in a way that reveals what has perhaps been lost or overlooked. Our "dull, small, banal, quotidian" concerns were once uncharted territory. Wallace's philosophy in *The Pale King* (*TPK* 546) is that we can ride out waves of boredom and oblivion into bliss and conscious (re)discovery, like another pioneer. With respect to Wallace's fiction, as Don DeLillo said, "There is always another reader to regenerate these words" (DeLillo, *Legacy* 24).

Greg Carlisle

Good Old Neon

Consciousness in and of itself is not a cure for oblivion; awareness can lead inward to crippling self-absorption and feelings of fraudulence. But awareness can also lead outward to possibilities of extraordinary perspective. In "Good Old Neon," Wallace demonstrates these possibilities by documenting the explosion of nested perspectives that can occur in "a few seconds' silence's flood of thoughts" (p. 150).

1. THINGS I TRIED (PP. 141-143)

The opening sequence establishes the narrator's life-long struggle with fraudulence, trying "to create a certain impression of me in other people. Mostly to be liked or admired." Several themes resonant with *Infinite Jest* are introduced. Like Hal, the narrator struggles with a need for approval from a very early age, and his "neon aura" (p. 180) is like Hal's "halo of approved grace" (*IJ* 999n76). Like some Ennet residents, the narrator's "circle of people" is "contemptuous of clichés." Like other Ennet residents, who want to stop taking substances but can't stop, the narrator "was disgusted with myself for always being such a fraud, but I couldn't seem to help it." By the end of the sequence, Wallace has prepared us for his nested, all-at-once narratives. The narrator will provide us with details of his life of fraudulence and simultaneously will provide us with perspective on that life of fraudulence from the vantage point of his afterlife. The list of things the narrator tried to combat fraudulence, many of which will be discussed in his analyst's office, appears to be sequential; but analysis, "pretty much the last thing" he tried, is in the middle of the list. Even though in life the narrator tried things one at a time, from the perspective of his afterlife they can be considered "all at once" in a "flash like neon" (p. 179, third and fifth lines from the bottom of the note).

2. THE BIG INSIGHT AND QUESTION I REALIZED I'D SET MYSELF UP FOR (PP. 143-147)

The narrator describes the décor of his analyst Dr. Gustafson's office. He twice reiterates that he knows what his problem is, but that he can't stop. Like Hal, the narrator leads his analyst "around by the nose" at first; but unlike Hal, the narrator later admits to his analyst "some of the ways I'd been jerking him around." As the analyst prepares to catch the narrator in the "logical contradiction or paradox" of being "honest about the fraudulence," the narrator delays the analyst's question (a significant moment and turning point in the narrator's attitude toward his analyst while alive) for seven pages, briefly returning to the office décor before going on two longer narrative tangents.

3. THE FRAUD PART OF ME WAS ALWAYS THERE (PP. 147-150)

At age nineteen, the narrator became aware of the "fraudulence paradox" (described on p. 147) and discovered that "being a fraud was a vicious infinite regress that ultimately resulted in being frightened, lonely, alienated, etc." But even with his newfound awareness, he couldn't stop being a fraud. In fact, his discovery "brought home" to him "what an empty, fraudulent person" he'd been since at least age four when he realized that if he admitted in a "clumsy, implausible way" that he'd broken a glass bowl, then he wouldn't be believed and his sister Fern would be blamed. This realization "suddenly hit" him "in a flash" and made him feel "suddenly connected to something larger." But it's a surface, selfish connection: note the use of a 2-D puzzle analogy by a narrator who "looked and acted

Greg Carlisle

much better on the surface then than Fern did." The narrator failed to understand the depth of the situation; he "neglected to anticipate" his sister's reaction and her subsequent punishment for telling the truth that her parents didn't believe, putting her in a situation that was "horrible," "possibly one of the worst feelings in the world."

4. ALL THESE TOTAL MISUNDERSTANDINGS OF WHAT'S REALLY GOING ON (PP. 150-153)

Conscious of his digression from Dr. Gustafson's impending question, the narrator assures the reader "that all of this and more was flashing through my head just in the interval of the small, dramatic pause Dr. Gustafson allowed himself." The narrator asserts that "many of the most important impressions and thoughts in a person's life are ones that flash through your head so fast . . . they seem . . . outside of the regular sequential clock time we all live by." (Compare this with what the narrator of "The Soul Is Not a Smithy" says on p. 97: "the most vivid and enduring occurrences in our lives are often those that occur at the periphery of our awareness.") Our narrator further asserts that these thoughts "have so little relation to the sort of linear, one-word-after-another-word English we all communicate with each other with that it could easily take a whole lifetime just to spell out the contents of one split-second's flash of thoughts and connections." And so he says of our use of language: "deep down everybody knows it's a charade." "What goes on inside is just too fast and huge and all interconnected for words to do more than just barely sketch the outlines of at most one tiny little part of it at any given instant." "Words and chronological time create all these total misunderstandings of what's really going on at the most basic level. And yet at the same time English is all we have to try and understand it and try to form anything larger or more meaningful and true with anybody else, which is yet another paradox."

What's really going on is expressed or hinted at by the narrator throughout this section. He discusses his post-death relationships with both time and Dr. Gustafson. He confirms that the experience of "people's whole life flashing before their eyes as they're dying isn't all that far off," but notes that "*whole life* isn't really a sequential thing" and that "it all happens at once, but that *at once* doesn't mean a finite moment of sequential time." Even "the term *my life* isn't even close to what we think we're talking about," as evidenced by the narrator's post-death meeting with Dr. Gustafson, who "had almost nothing to do with" the analyst the narrator knew in life (cf. "I'm not sure I remember him alive too well," p. 143). After noting "the really central, overarching paradox" of using sequential words to call into question the use of sequential words (that we're hearing from a supposedly dead narrator who considered himself a fraud his whole life), the narrator informs us that "we're sitting here in this car" with him and that his narrative is partially for the benefit of our having "at least some idea" of why his death "had the impact it did on who this is really about." On my first reading, I didn't realize I was sitting in a car and that the narrative was not really about the narrator. The narrator notes "how clumsy and laborious it seems to be to convey even the smallest thing."

5. WHAT IT WAS LIKE INSIDE MY HEAD (PP. 153-155)

We return after seven pages, "the tiny interval between then and now," to Dr. Gustafson, leaning back in his chair and preparing to deliver "his big logical insight" to the narrator in the form of a question. But first, the narrator thinks briefly of Fern and asserts, in language that resonates with the philosophy espoused in *Infinite Jest*'s AA meetings, "that we're all lonely, of

Greg Carlisle

course. Everyone knows this, it's almost a cliché. So yet another layer of my essential fraudulence is that I pretended to myself that my loneliness was special . . . . It's not special at all, we've all got it."

Wallace now treats us to a feast of layered paradoxes that illustrates "how exhausting and solipsistic" it is to be like the narrator was. Dr. Gustafson asks the narrator (whose "given name," we learn, is Neal) how, if he is unable to be honest, he was able to be honest with Dr. Gustafson "a moment ago." The question disappoints the narrator because "the real truth was that my confession of being a fraud . . . had itself been kind of manipulative" and because Dr. Gustafson's insight, given the narrator's logic on p. 154, "was not only obvious and superficial but also wrong." ("A corollary to the fraudulence paradox is that you simultaneously want to fool everyone you meet and yet also somehow always hope that you'll come across someone who is your match or equal and can't be fooled.") And but then the narrator follows this by saying that the "unspoken point of the analyst's insight—namely, that who and what I believed I was was not what I really was at all—which I thought was false, was in fact true, although not for the reasons Dr. Gustafson . . . believed."

6. THIS FOG OF FRAUDULENCE (PP. 155-158)

Fraudulently, the narrator continues to see Dr. Gustafson even though he has given up on him and is considering suicide, countering the doctor's "upbeat diagnosis" "by means of listing [he spares giving us "the whole list again," cf. pp. 142-3] the various ways [he'd] been fraudulent even in [his] pursuit of ways to achieve genuine and uncalculating integrity." In this section, Wallace associates fraudulence with oblivion: as early as age fourteen, the narrator retreats from pleasant awareness of external stimuli associated with playing ball into internal, self-obsessed worrying about playing ball that makes him feel like he is "actually asleep and none of this [is] even real." He becomes less conscious of external stimuli, oblivious. Ironing his uniform gives him "too much time to think," and he doesn't notice the sounds and smells associated with ironing anymore. This eventually leads the narrator to try various things like joining a church "to wake up spiritually instead of living in this fog of fraudulence."

Wallace initiates the narrator's discussion of the church with a reference to fish in water and ties that image to the iconic Christian fish. Wallace's iconic motif (in *This Is Water*) of fish oblivious to the fact that they are in water resonates with the narrator's lack of awareness, his conning himself, in this section. Wallace keeps his focus on the narrator and does not overtly suggest that the parishioners of the charismatic church are in a state of mutually-supportive group oblivion with respect to their beliefs, but contrast this passage with the passage in "Another Pioneer" in which the child ponders group mimicry, "putative belief," and feelings of fraudulence (p. 133).

The narrator experiences a sudden "flash of self-awareness" in which he realizes that he just wanted everyone to think he was sincere. The narrator has been "genuinely . . . struck" ("It just about knocked me over"), whereas before, his falling after being popped by his pastor was not genuine. The narrator notes an escalation in fraudulence, because "before the church thing" he had "been able to admit and face the fraudulence directly instead of B.S.ing myself that I was something I wasn't."

7. WARNINGS FROM MY SUBCONSCIOUS (PP. 158-162)

The narrator now reminds us that he is manipulating Dr. Gustafson and (recalling the inadequacies of words and chronological time discussed earlier) that he is only telling us

Greg Carlisle

"about some of the more garish examples" of his fraudulence because the "very long pseudo-argument . . . would take way too much time to relate to [us] in detail." After a brief mention of fraudulence with respect to jogging, the narrator recounts his fraudulence with respect to his meditation class: he could only "sit and appear quiet and mindful and withstand the unbelievably restless and horrible feelings when . . . there were other people to make [a false] impression on." But don't we assume that people are paying much more attention to us than they actually are? The people in the dream triggered by the narrator's teacher Master Gurpreet's dubbing him "the statue" take no notice of the narrator's exertions. The dream "takes place in dream time as opposed to waking, chronological time." "And in the dream my whole life flashes by like that, the sun and moon go back and forth across the sky like windshield wipers over and over." The repetition of daily life is a motif of Wallace's in *Infinite Jest* and *This Is Water*, and dreams are often significant and ominous, as in *Infinite Jest* and the titular story of this collection.

8. A VIRTUAL HALL OF MIRRORS (P. 162)

The last two sections were similarly structured: a reminder of the narrator's manipulation of Dr. Gustafson, an announcement of a time-saving choice, a brief example of fraudulence, a longer example of fraudulence. The narrator indicates that he could continue in this fashion: the section begins with "Etc., etc. I'll spare you any more examples" and then hints at how much further into fraudulence he could go by describing his "fraudulence with girls" for three lines and fraudulence in his career ("manipulating people's images of your ability to manipulate images, a virtual hall of mirrors") for the rest of the paragraph. Wallace simultaneously has his narrator continue a narrative progression (the narrator referred to girls with whom he was fraudulent and to his career in the previous section) and pull back from the narrative center of sections 2-7 (Dr. Gustafson's office) to return to the subject of the first section: girls with whom he was fraudulent and his career.

9. ALL THE WAY THROUGH TO THE CORE (PP. 162-164)

In the flash of a line break, Wallace shifts the primary focus of his narrative from an analysis of the narrator's fraudulence and the inadequacies of language to the nested nature of consciousness and the impossibility of living human beings to move "outside linear time" into a perspective of selfless objectivity. From this higher level of consciousness, the narrator now frames Dr. Gustafson's previously-described behavior and office decor as symbolic representations of the analyst's "major sexual insecurities." Dr. Gustafson attributes the narrator's inability to acknowledge his "ability to be genuine" to "insecurities or male fears" prompted by the "brainwashing" of "America's culture." (The first part of "Good Old Neon" began with a list of things the narrator tried to combat fraudulence; this part begins with Dr. Gustafson's list of the "damaging beliefs and superstitions" of American male culture.)

Another shift is that instead of just acknowledging an awareness of fraudulence, the afterlife narrator now analyzes what he should have done to combat the fraudulence: "If I'd had an ounce of real self-respect I would have . . . gone back . . . and thrown myself on Master Gurpreet's mercy, since . . . he was the only one who'd appeared to see all the way through to the core of my fraudulence." But the living narrator didn't do this. Even though he was consciously manipulating Dr. Gustafson, he still "conned" himself into thinking that by seeing Dr. Gustafson he was "finding a way to be genuine and stop manipulating everybody around [him] to see 'the statue' as erect

Greg Carlisle

and impressive, etc." (Note that the narrator's choice of adjectives here might lend credence to Dr. Gustafson's theories about American culture "brainwashing its males.")

10. It penetrated (pp. 164-166)

Dr. Gustafson claims that love and fear are mutually exclusive and that American men live "in a more or less constant state of fear that [makes] genuine love next to impossible." The narrator uses a complex equation of formal logic in this section to heighten the sense of cold objectivity and higher levels of perception, of distance. Upon hearing Dr. G's claim, "the idea struck me that maybe the real root of my problem was not fraudulence but a basic inability to really love." This prompts a memory of Beverly-Elizabeth Slane, who communicated to our narrator that "she'd never felt the gaze of someone so penetrating, discerning, and yet totally empty of care, like she was a puzzle or problem." Referring to this, our narrator says "it penetrated, I never did forget what she said in that letter." The narrator's perception of his emotional distance from Slane is underscored in the narrative by the physical distance of communication via letter instead of a face-to-face meeting.

11. There's a before and an after, and afterward you're different (pp. 166-169)

The narrator's new perception of potentially being unable to love gives him "a different model or lens through which to see [his] problem" and "a promising way of attacking the fraudulence paradox." He says, "This period was pretty much the zenith of my career in analysis, and for a few weeks . . . I felt some of the first genuine hope I'd had since the early, self-deluded part" of his time with the charismatic church. (The ellipsis of the previous hopeful sentence omits a 9-line parenthetical description of Dr. G's physical decline.) "And yet at the same time these weeks also led more or less directly to my decision to kill myself."

The narrator is again at pains to have us understand the timelessness of "the sudden internal flash when you see or realize something" and disclaims that he is "going to have to simplify and linearize a great deal of interior stuff in order to convey to [us] what actually happened." He says it would be best to express his insights in terms of logical symbolism "because logic is totally abstract and outside what we think of as time." But even a statement of objective logic can be crippled by a higher level of perception. The narrator cites Berry's paradox that *the very smallest number that can't be described in under twenty-two syllables* is described in the twenty-one syllables of the preceding italicized phrase.

One night in August 1991, the narrator "happened on part of an old *Cheers* episode" (the sitcom also has a significant place in Don Gately's remembrances of childhood in *Infinite Jest*) in which a remark by the analyst character Lilith caused him to recognize "what a cliché and melodramatic type of complaint the inability-to-love concept was." In a flash, the narrator simultaneously realizes that he had "managed to con" himself with respect to his battle with fraudulence, that he had "deluded" himself with respect to Dr. G's ability to help him, and that "nearly everybody in the United States had probably already seen through the complaint's inauthenticity." This realization "more of less destroyed" him, and he woke up the next morning "having decided" he was going to kill himself. What appeared to be a definitive statement about a higher order number turned out not to be definitive. What appeared to be a sequential move toward resolving the fraudulence problem produced no movement toward resolution. Wallace

Greg Carlisle

underscores this lack of sequential movement through time by having the narrator remind us that we are still in a car with him and that he died in 1991.

12. THERE ARE THINGS YOU CAN DISCUSS IN A SUICIDE NOTE (PP. 170-173)

The narrator spends his last morning writing notes to people and assessing the level of fraudulence in the notes. He apologizes to his employers "for in any way leaving them in the lurch," but the "note was probably ultimately just so that the people who really mattered at [work] would be more apt to remember me as a decent, conscientious guy." He chooses not to write to Dr. Gustafson, because he "knew that in the note I'd spend a lot of time trying to seem as if I was being honest but really just dancing around the truth." He also wrote a note to his sister Fern, apologizing for the glass bowl incident and "other incidents and spiteful or fraudulent actions that I knew had caused her pain and that I had felt bad about ever since, but had never really seen any way to broach with her or express honest regret for." He warns Fern that he has "probably deliberately constructed the note to at least in part prompt" her likely initial reaction.

13. I'D SOMEHOW CHOSEN TO CAST MY LOT WITH MY LIFE'S DRAMA'S SUPPOSED AUDIENCE INSTEAD OF WITH THE DRAMA ITSELF (PP. 173-176)

The narrator intensifies the narrative by stating that "we're getting to the part where I actually kill myself." But Wallace's story is really about the complex nature and nested levels of human consciousness, so the narrator opines about this for three pages before taking us to the site of his death. On one level the narrator experiences "the sacredness of the world as seen," sensory experiences and remembrances rich in specific detail and voluminous: only "about one one-trillionth of the various thoughts and internal experiences I underwent in those last few hours" are documented on pp. 172-3. Simultaneously, the narrator realizes "that everything he sees will outlast him," that we are "just instruments or expressions of our evolutionary drives, which are themselves the expressions of forces that are infinitely larger and more important than we are." "As a verbal construction I know that's a cliché. As a state in which to actually be, though, it's something else, believe me."

Wallace takes his narrator through several levels of consciousness in the extraordinary page-length sentence of pp. 175-6. Writing his note to Fern, the narrator was 1) "expressing sentiments and regrets that were real" while simultaneously 2) "noticing what a fine and sincere note it was, and anticipating the effect on Fern of this or that heartfelt phrase, while yet another part was [3)] observing the whole scene . . . thinking what a fine and genuine-seeming performance in a drama it would make [3a)] if only we had not already been subjected to countless scenes just like it . . . which somehow entailed that real scenes like the one of my suicide note were now compelling and interesting only to their participants . . . [3b)] which is somewhat paradoxical [given] that the reason scenes like this will seem stale and manipulative to an audience is that we've already seen so many of them in dramas, [3c)] and yet the reason we've seen so many of them in dramas is that the scenes really are dramatic and compelling and let people communicate very deep, complicated emotional realities that are almost impossible to articulate in any other way, and at the same time still another facet or part of me [4) was] realizing . . . I'd somehow chosen to cast my lot with my life's drama's supposed audience instead of with the drama itself, and that I even now was watching and gauging my supposed performance's quality

Greg Carlisle

and probable effects, and thus [5)] was in the final analysis the very same manipulative fraud writing the note to Fern that I had been throughout the life that had brought me to this climactic scene of writing and signing" and sending it on the way to kill himself.

14. The universes inside you (pp. 176-180)

The narrator's journey through abstract consciousness has brought us back full circle to concrete descriptions rich in sensory detail in this section. The journey is not without its lessons: realizing his tendency to play to a supposed audience, the narrator crafts his suicide to have "as little an aspect of performance" to it as he can manage. As he drives, insects "rise up out of the fields like some great figure's shadow rising" (a shadow symbolizes ominous import here as well as throughout *Infinite Jest*), the "whole insect universe in there that none of us will ever see or know anything about" (cf. "Electric sounds of insects at their business" and "Insects all business all the time" on p. 3 of *The Pale King*). The narrator asserts that we all want to know "what it's like to die," so much so that we, in the car with the narrator, apparently are considering whether "to go through with it or not" and think the narrator is going to try to talk us out of it.

But he says that we "already know what it's like," that we "already know the difference between the size and speed of everything that flashes through you and the tiny inadequate bit of it all you can ever let anybody know. As though inside you is this enormous room full of what seems like everything in the whole universe at one time or another and yet the only parts that get out have to somehow squeeze out" through "tiny keyholes." And what if "afterward, after what you think of as *you* has died" "the universes inside you" are "somehow fully open and expressible" "and you don't even need any organized

English, you can as they say open the door and be in anyone else's room in all your own multiform forms and ideas and facets?" He scoffs at the idea that we might consider ourselves to be simply some "sum or remainder" of the "millions and trillions of thoughts, memories, juxtapositions" that flash through our heads and asserts that "Of course you're a fraud, of course" "the tiny fraction anyone else ever sees" of you "is never you." This is "why it feels so good to break down and cry in front of others, or to laugh, or speak in tongues, or chant in Bengali—it's not English anymore, it's not getting squeezed through any hole."

    The narrator asks us if we know "how long it's been since I told you I was a fraud" (since the opening sentence of the story) and suggests that "no time has passed at all," which is true because p. 141 of this book is in our hands at the exact same time that p. 179 is. We are asked, in a footnote that seems to be Wallace popping into the car with us for a brief extra-narrative aside (the narrator would not say "nice car by the way" because he is in his own car with "the RESPICEM watch hanging from the rearview" which refers to the narrator's "stepmother's . . . silver pocketwatch . . . with the Latin RESPICE FINEM inscribed" on it (p. 161) which translates as "look to the end" or "consider the outcome" which is a funny thing to put on a watch that either runs in a cycle that never ends or is stopped and does not move), "What if there's really no movement at all?" What if "not only your whole life but every single humanly conceivable way to describe and account for that life has time to flash like neon . . . through your mind all at once in the literally immeasurable instant between impact and death"? The phrase "THE END" can only occur in this footnote outside the narrative proper because the narrative itself happens in an "immeasurable instant." It cannot end; it is a timeless, all-at-once "flash like neon."

Continuing to blur or discount the concept of sequential time, the narrator doesn't say of our impending suicide that it *won't make* you a fraud to change your mind but rather that it *wouldn't have made* you a fraud to change your mind, as if our suicide has already occurred, like his. But then he says, "It would be sad to do it because you think you somehow have to," because we would be basing our fraudulence on the faulty premise that we are only the "tiny fraction" of ourselves that other people see.

15. THROUGH THE TINY LITTLE KEYHOLE OF HIMSELF (PP. 180-181)

The narrator asserts that understanding the paradoxes of his narrative is "a matter of perspective" and then proceeds, in yet another expansion of consciousness, to describe five other perspectives occurring in "the very same instant" that "this whole seemingly endless back-and-forth between us has come and gone and come again." The sequence concludes with David Wallace, who "blinks in the midst of idly scanning class photos from his 1980 Aurora West H.S. yearbook and seeing my photo and trying, through the tiny little keyhole of himself, to imagine what all must have happened to lead up to my death in the fiery single-car accident he'd read about in 1991." And now we know "who this is really about" (p. 152). "Good Old Neon" is the document of David Wallace, in the blink on an eye, "happening to have a huge and totally unorganizable set of inner thoughts, feelings, memories and impressions of this little photo's guy a year ahead of him in school with the seemingly almost neon aura": good old Neal, who is indeed a fraud because his narration comes not from his own mind but from the mind of David Wallace (who has Neal report from his afterlife that death "won't hurt" while he imagines that it is "doubtlessly painful") speculating about him (see Figure 7). The same charge of fraudulence can be lodged against any character written by any author. "Good Old Neon" celebrates the necessarily fraudulent art of fiction and the all-at-once, neon flash of creativity.

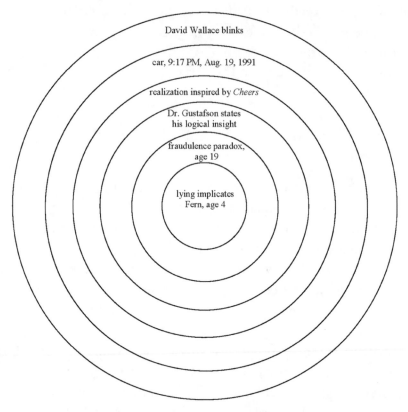

David Wallace blinks

car, 9:17 PM, Aug. 19, 1991

realization inspired by *Cheers*

Dr. Gustafson states
his logical insight

fraudulence paradox,
age 19

lying implicates
Fern, age 4

Figure 7. A partial diagram of David Wallace's flash of thoughts representing nested flashes of realization and moments of significance for Neal all the way back to age 4

While celebrating the complexities of human consciousness, "Good Old Neon" also warns of its self-centered tendencies. The story concludes with David Wallace "fully aware that the cliché that you can't ever truly know what's going on inside somebody else is hoary and insipid and yet at the same time trying very consciously to prohibit that awareness from mocking the attempt . . . commanding that other part to be silent as if looking it levelly in the eye and saying, almost aloud, 'Not another word,'" which, appropriately, are the last words of the story. The eccentric, bracketed (because they are not spoken by Neal) symbols that follow are presumably for or to (cf. the arrow) Neal and represent his initials, year of graduation, and batting average. Given that we are at the limit of expressing the boundaries of human consciousness, the last words of the story also recall the famous last words of Wittgenstein's *Tractatus Logico-Philosophicus*: "Whereof we cannot speak, thereof we must be silent."

"Good Old Neon" is an excellent example of Wallace's wish to make fiction that is "about what it is to be a fucking *human being*" (McCaffery 26), for here he has his protagonist pull back out of the narrative (taking us with him) to look at his creator creating him. Far from simply being a metafictional trick, Wallace does this to signal that the story is an attempt to understand another human being (presumably Wallace is basing this story on someone he actually knew).

The "sacredness of the world as seen" in "Good Old Neon" is analogous to the bliss on the other side of boredom in *The Pale King*, which, like "Good Old Neon," features a character named after its author. "Good Old Neon" asserts that because we are limited in our ability to express ourselves, we cannot escape fraudulence any more than we can escape the strictures of language and time. But we can experience a neon flash of awareness, a blissful creative moment, an escape from the crippling self-consciousness of boredom. We can choose to silence mocking thoughts when experiencing a flash of other-directed awareness, to look out through the tiny little keyholes of ourselves, to experience the sacredness of the world as seen.

Philosophy and the Mirror of Nature

Like "Incarnations of Burned Children" and "Another Pioneer," this is a single-paragraph story. Like "The Soul Is Not a Smithy" the story's title is an allusion to another text: in this case, Richard Rorty's seminal philosophical work. In his book, Rorty discredits the philosophical notion of comparing the mind to a mirror that reflects nature and suggests that "If we see knowing not as having an essence, to be described by scientists and philosophers, but rather as a right, by current standards, to believe, then we are well on the way to seeing *conversation* as the ultimate context within which knowledge is to be understood" (Rorty 389). Justifying or adapting our beliefs in conversation with others is a better model of reality than solipsistically looking into the "mirrors" of our minds. Wallace's characters highlight the fact that we resist adapting our beliefs, that we fear the potentially negative reactions of others, and that we feel the pull of the isolating comfort of our mirror-gazing.

A mirror provides a surface reflection with the illusion of depth; but what we see can be misleading, because the reality of a moment is influenced by events and experiences outside the mirror's frame. Wallace begins by establishing a linear progression of the chain of events (the narrative threads) that bear upon the moment of his story. It's just a scaffold, though, so it's up to us to arrange subsequent narrative details on this scaffold to determine for ourselves the reality of the narrator's situation. We must listen carefully to the narrator, whose address to us toggles between all the narrative threads in seemingly random fashion.

The story begins in progress like "Another Pioneer." "Then just as I was being released in late 1996 [first narrative thread: what did he do?] Mother won a small product liability settlement [second narrative thread: what happened?] and used the money to promptly go get ["botched"] cosmetic surgery . . . which caused her to look *insanely frightened* at all times. . . . So then she went and had more ["also botched"] cosmetic surgery . . . and the appearance of fright became even worse." Events associated with the first surgery constitute the third narrative thread, and events associated with the second surgery constitute the fourth narrative thread. Wallace's technique of italicizing short phrases throughout this story (he does this in a few sections of *Infinite Jest*, too) recalls Rorty's technique of putting quotes around short phrases throughout his book. Note how easily the observer can be misled: the narrator's mother looks insanely frightened, but in reality she is not. Note also that in describing how his mother looked after each surgery, the narrator refers to two iconic film moments which, although fictional, "let people communicate very deep, complicated emotional realities that are almost impossible to articulate in any other way" ("Good Old Neon," p. 176; cf. also the narrator of "The Soul Is Not a Smithy" on an iconic moment from *The Exorcist*, pp. 94-97). Describing the present situation, the narrator says of his mother, "So now she was involved in still another lawsuit and when she regularly took the bus to the attorney she had chosen's office [fifth narrative thread], I would *escort her*."

The narrator describes how he and his mother sit on the bus in such a way as to avoid the reactions of passengers to his mother's appearance and to his: he is quite tall and wears goggles and gloves. The narrator has "a studious bend" and uses phrases like "experimental method," "habitat," and "specimen," the latter to refer to both himself and to the objects of his "field work." Referring to his mother's status as his post-probation custodian, the narrator says that "reality was the other way around because due to despondency and fear of others' reactions to [the second surgery] she is all but incapable of leaving the house." As the narrative progresses, we will learn that "fear of others' reactions" and/or "fear of the phylum *arthropodae*" (a recurring source of fear in *Infinite Jest*, too) are root causes of all the disastrous (or potentially disastrous) events described in the narrative threads (see Figure 8).

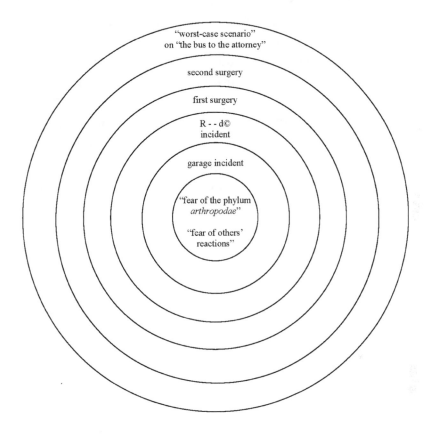

Figure 8. Nested disasters or potential disasters
and associated core fears

Wallace signals an upgrade in narrative complexity by having the narrator zoom in on the bus driver at his steering wheel at p. 184, line 9. Now that this intensification of detail in the fifth thread (bus ride) has our attention, Wallace shifts without warning into the first thread (garage incident) at line 15 and then toggles abruptly between these two threads for about a page before weaving the third thread (first surgery) back in at p. 185, line 2 and the second thread (R - - d© incident) back in at p. 185, line 24. (Note that Wallace, a fierce champion of the serial comma, has his narrator omit a serial comma twice: "state, county or local ordinance" at p. 184, line 17; and "vain, bitter and timid female specimen" at p. 185, line 7.)

It takes a few pages of text to piece together the reality of the garage incident. Reintroducing this thread (p. 184) with "Nor did I have anything against the boy" and phrases like "varieties you can study" and "reckless endangerment" seem to implicate our narrator as responsible for an ominous deed. But it turns out the boy fell through the narrator's garage roof onto spiders that were "carefully contained and screened off and even the state conceded that if [the boy] had not been fiddling around on the roof of someone else's garage there is no way he could have come in contact with them." But reality is influenced by many factors, by many voices in conversation: the boy "was only nine which was repeatedly stressed as if his age in any way strengthened any charge of negligence" on the narrator's part. Given that it was "due to the [boy's] mishap" that "some partial decontainment and penetration of the surrounding neighborhood" by the spiders occurred, the narrator does not believe he failed "due exercise of caution," especially given the reality that "any environs as unkempt as our surrounding neighborhood will already be naturally infested with them."

Greg Carlisle

So you would think the narrator, falsely charged with negligence and disparaging of lawyers, might have qualms about escorting his mother to a "negligence specialist" (p. 187, reintroduction of second surgery thread). But the narrator's loyalty to his mother ("I'm all the support she has") aligns his perception of reality with hers, and that perception may be suspect. Consider the details of the narrator's mother's disastrous incidents. We learn near the end of the story that her "original liability was that a worker at the assembly plant actually glued a can's nozzle on facing backward, [a] condition of the settlement being to never mention the trade name of the common household spray in any connection to the liability suit, which I am resolved to honor on her behalf." This explains the narrator's omission of letters earlier when referencing his mother's "constant spraying of R - - d©" (Wallace makes the omission of letters a consistent trait by having his narrator omit letters in his imagined reaction on p. 189—*What the f - - k are you looking at*—symbolic of Wallace's technique of having us fill in narrative blanks throughout this story). But regardless of where the nozzle is on the can, we point it away from us before spraying, and even if we didn't wouldn't the spray hit our hands? Even the narrator says his mother's "*pain and suffering* appeared somewhat inflated in the original product liability claim and in reality she coughs less than during her own deposition."

After "the first surgery's bandages came off," the narrator's mother "could not herself ascertain at first if the look of insane terror was the response or the stimulus and if it was a response then a response to what in the mirror if the response itself was the expression." The mirror is not an accurate measure of reality. The narrator suggests that the surgeon's "leaning against the wall with his face to the wall" signaled that "there was an objective problem in the surgery's results," but surely the surgeon might just be in despair over a potential lawsuit given the narrator's mother's irrational but hard-to-refute claim with respect to his work. And are we seriously to believe a second surgery was also botched?

Knowledge and truth are the products of conversation, of what rational speakers can persuade other rational listeners to believe by presenting multiple perspectives on particular issues or events. Conversation requires social engagement, talking-with rather than talking-at, a willingness to accept the tension and resistance to easy resolution of human interaction. Our narrator is isolated and distant. He uses film imagery to describe his mother, effective in that the images are common to a large number of people but also impersonal. His vocabulary is dominated by clinical terms. He imagines conversations rather than having them. In fact, he positions himself on the bus in such a way as to avoid conversations. He is on the defensive, sees himself as his mother's protector ("her sematic accessory or escort"), and prepares for a "worst-case scenario" against "hostile organisms" and "potential predators." (With the appearance of the "black jointed foreleg" on p. 189, we learn why the narrator's briefcase was referenced as "a *sematic accessory* to warn off potential predators" on p. 184.) But isolation breeds aggression and fear and mistrust. "Recluses" exhibit "*a native aggression*"; and widows, if disturbed, have a maximally painful bite. "Mother is blackly cynical in matters of the heart referring to the entire spectrum of mating rituals as *a disaster waiting to happen*."

It takes more than awareness, more than a "studious bend," to escape the oblivion of solipsistic isolation. Awareness is more than self-assessment and mirror-gazing and facts derived from a single perspective. We escape oblivion by choosing what we pay attention to (as Fogle will tell us in §22 of *The Pale King*) and by risking the disaster waiting to happen (like

Greg Carlisle

Lane Dean Jr. seems about to do in §6 of *The Pale King*). The mirror more aptly symbolizes oblivion than reality, a heightened awareness of which must be attained through action, by choosing what to pay attention to and what to believe, persuading and justifying and reassessing in myriad threads of evolving conversations.

Oblivion

In this story, Wallace crafts an environment of oblivion by putting us inside the mind of a dreamer anxious about "knowing whether or not I am asleep . . . . To doubt this would be the road to insanity." Memories or fears of sexual abuse, repressed or denied when waking, are manifest in the story, which Wallace reveals to be a dream on the last page. But there are several motifs throughout the text that in hindsight (or on a second reading) suggest the experiences or thought-processes of the dreamer.

1. IN SOME SUBTLE BUT UNMISTAKABLE WAY, 'OFF' (PP. 190-198)

Our narrator, Randall Napier, sits out a storm with his wife Hope's stepfather, Dr. Sipe, in the clubhouse of the golf course of which Randall is a member. Sipe dismisses Napier's attempt to broach the subject of "the strange and absurdly frustrating marital conflict between Hope and myself over the issue of my so-called 'snoring,'" and prepares to smoke "an expensive Cohiba cigar."

One motif in this story that occasionally jars the reader out of narrative for a split-second (resonant with a dreamer's occasional split-second feelings that "something's not quite right here" throughout the dream) is Randall's erroneous or eccentric usage and punctuation. He occasionally misuses the reflexive pronoun "myself" (beginning on p. 190, line 1; cf. Sally Foster Wallace, pp. 103-4). He frequently puts single quotation marks around words or phrases, not just to define or call attention to them, but also to call into question their accuracy or appropriateness (beginning with "'front' nine" on p. 190, line 2); this quirk gives Napier the quality of an obsessive questioner with a need for precision, which resonates with the desperation of one who seeks to prove on which side of the waking/dreaming boundary they lie. He occasionally hyphenates words that are no longer hyphenated and capitalizes words that do not need capitalization (like "Club-house" on p. 190, line 3). He frequently omits serial commas before the last item of a series (beginning with three instances on p. 193; cf. Sally Foster Wallace, p. 41). He substitutes backslashes for slashes, as in "and\or" on p. 193.

One of several other motifs is Napier's irritation with Sipe: Sipe's air of "'triumphant' grievance," his insistence on taking his non-member-stickered car to the club, and his "referring once more to [his] watch's retail price" (pp. 190-1). There are several instances of paired names: the waitress Audrey Bogen and "our own Audrey" Napier; her father Jack Bogen and Jack Vivien, whose actual name is Chester (p. 214), which is also the name of Hope's brother (p. 195). Hope has sisters named Vivian (p. 207) and Meredith (p. 191), and her stepfather's name is Edmund (p. 196); Randall's therapist is named Ed (p. 209); and Hope and Randall attend the Edmund R. and Meredith R. Darling Sleep Clinic. As in a dream, there is an undercurrent of sexual imagery or symbols in the story, which in nearly every instance indicates inappropriateness or abuse: Sipe looks at "the young, voluptuous waitress's face," and "Randy" Napier struggles not to look at "the nubile adolescents in our own Audrey's peer circle." Both Sipe and Napier are stepfathers, and there are suggestions of inappropriateness with respect to the children in their care. Sipe's appearance is often characterized as threatening; he appears "to be thrusting his face and mouth [which continues to move after he speaks] forward directly at one in an aggressive, almost predatory fashion."

Greg Carlisle

Wallace establishes a motif of dreamlike environmental distortion by having Napier's "nearly seven months of severe sleep disturbance" prompt "disorientation" and "distorted or 'altered' sensory perception" in which colors brighten and "the visual environment appeared to faintly pulse and throb, and individual objects appeared, paradoxically, both to recede and become far-away and at the same time to come into an unnatural visual focus" (this dual quality is also a recurrent motif in *Infinite Jest*). Napier also experiences hallucinations, beginning with "an endlessly ringing and unanswered public telephone" on p. 194. Words or phrases that pierce the dream from outside are initiated here with "For God's sake" and "*up*" in the last line of p. 196 (cf. pp. 211, 222, 232, and 237). Long digressions that keep us from reaching the end of the dream are initiated here too with the 13½-line parenthetical digression on p. 196. By p. 197, "no more than five or six minutes had passed."

2. CONFABULATING PAST AND PRESENT AND TRUTH AND DREAM (PP. 198-204)

The "present marital conflict is that I [Randall], in reality, am not yet truly even asleep at the times my wife cries out suddenly now about my 'snoring' and disturbing her nearly every night since our Audrey's departure from home." "Since the prior Autumn," Hope "steadfastly avows" that Randall's "putative 'snoring' is a waking reality instead of her own dream." Hope, using her sister "Vivian (. . . to whom Hope was extremely close before their 'falling out')'s lexicon," accuses Randall of "being 'in denial,' an accusation any denial of which was held, of course, to be evidence in its own favor, maddeningly." This foreshadowing of Vivian's equally un- provable accusations (presumably of sexual abuse at the hands of Sipe, cf. pp. 207 and 214) occurs a page after reference to a piercing telephone ring and just before the word "saffron" is tied to Audrey Napier. Recall "the incongruous odor of saffron" that accompanied the hallucination of the endlessly ringing telephone on p. 194. Randall, "exiled" from his own bed by Hope, "got scarcely one iota or 'wink' of sleep the entire night in Audrey's former bed." Randall eventually begins "pantomiming a deeply sleeping man" until Hope goes back to sleep, but "sometimes she now once again bolts awake moments later."

3. THE ROAD TO INSANITY (PP. 204-210)

As the thunderstorm recedes, Sipe continues to run "the fine cigar over his upper lip in order to savor the aroma." Randall describes letting slip to Hope his secret visit to an Ear, Nose, and Throat specialist, which Hope sees as evidence that Randall "'. . . kn[e]w the snoring [was] real'" (these brackets are Wallace's, who often has his characters repeat other characters verbatim, using brackets to change the tense and remind the reader that the original statement is now in the mouth of a different character). The conflict between Randall and Hope escalates, causing Randall to lose sleep and begin having hallucinations due to sleep deprivation.

Randall's next step (pp. 207-10) is to see, without Hope, "a professional Couple counselor [here Wallace inserts a 15½-line em-dash digression which includes a nested 8 ½ -line parenthetical digression in which is buried Vivian's accusation] only [to] suffer or endure a series of 'therapeutic' exchanges" in which the counselor exasperates Randall by questioning rather than validating his statements. Shortly after the disturbing reference to Hope's "daughterly charms" (cf. the same phrase in reference to Audrey on p. 232), Randall says (and recall that we are currently inside a dream), "She's claiming to know better than I myself whether I'm even awake. It's less unfair than seemingly almost totally insane. I know whether I'm sitting

Greg Carlisle

here having these exchanges. I know I am not dreaming this. To doubt this is insane."

4. I KNOW WHEN I'M HALLUCINATING AND WHEN I'M NOT (PP. 210-219)

Randall has a hallucination of himself as a small child "standing precariously on a rise in the . . . great granite lap" of a "great, stone icon or statue," "clutching or grasping the end of [a] rope, peering up." The hallucination is influenced by events outside the dream. Randall experiences "a dominant or 'booming' voice . . . repeatedly commanding '*Up*' and the hand ["heavy upon my shoulder and back"] pushing or shaking and saying '*For God* . . .' and\or '. . . *Hope*' several times."

As Randall watches Sipe light his cigar, "the whole room seemed somehow menacingly coiled" (on p. 191 the room felt "over-confined, not unlike the lap of a dominant adult"). In a 25½-line parenthetical digression, Randall assures "a second Couple counselor" that he knows when he is hallucinating and when he is not by giving disturbing examples of his hallucinations, which include an image of Audrey Napier's breasts going "up and down in her sweater like pistons." Just after the digression, Randall has a "hallucinatory 'flash' or vision of our Audrey supine in a beached canoe and myself straining piston-like above her" which shifts into a vision of "our Audrey —now 19 and burgeoned into full woman-hood or the 'Age of consent'—in her familiar saffron bustier" doing Audrey Bogen's job at the 19th Hole Room in the clubhouse.

Just after this, Randall notes that "Jack Vivien was now there, as well, at the window-side table in the 19th Hole with myself and Dr. Sipe." Although Randall does not say that Vivien is a hallucination, he admits 1) that Vivien's being there, dry, "at this precise point in time is somewhat unclear and, in retrospect, contrived or, as it were, 'suspicious'"; 2) that it is "unlikely that Jack Vivien and Hope's stepfather knew one another"; and 3) that Sipe does not appear to "look at or in any way acknowledge the presence of Jack Vivien" (showing up with his "pudendal" facial hair just as Sipe lights his phallic cigar).

After Randall approached Vivien "the prior March" about his "conjugal 'snoring' impasse," Vivien "in late March, had subsequently suggested . . . the reportedly highly respected Edmund R. and Meredith R. Darling Sleep Clinic." (Let's digress for a moment to ponder the timeline of the narrative so far. At the time of his meeting with Sipe, Randall has experienced "nearly seven months of severe sleep disturbance." Audrey left for school "the prior Autumn," so late August or early September, which puts Vivien's suggestion in late March about seven months after that. Given that the Napiers have yet to go to the sleep clinic, where testing and diagnosis will take four weeks (cf. pp. 225-6), after which Randall decides to go to Sipe with the problem, we can assume it takes some period of time after Audrey's departure for Randall to begin characterizing his sleep deprivation as "severe." Also, Randall used the phrase "in retrospect" earlier, so presumably he is narrating to us from a point after his meeting with Sipe.)

Randall imagines that Sipe sees their meeting as one in which Randall is trying to ask Sipe "to use his paternal influence or authority over Hope . . . to intercede in the conflict." In that ellipsis triggered by Sipe's using his authority over Hope is a disturbing 11½-line digression in which Randall imagines that in Sipe's "pale eyes was what sometimes looked or appeared to be the terrible stepfatherly knowledge of what our Audrey could have been to me, perhaps as Hope . . . had once served as or been to himself" and in which Randall pictures Sipe presumably raping Hope or Vivian, "his crushing weight thoroughly and terribly adult." This is the last image of Sipe in the narrative.

Greg Carlisle

Jack Vivien helped Randall prepare to make his sleep-clinic proposal to Hope, whose "over-all mien has taken on a lupine or predatory aspect" in the eyes of Randall, who believes Hope projects her "grief" over the physical maturity of Audrey and her "comely peer circle" as "anger onto myself for merely owning eyes to see and be naturally affected by." Randall is "hard pressed to regard it as coincidental that all of these blossoming girls and daughters were, almost without exception, all dispatched to 'out-of-State' colleges, as with each passing year the mere physical sight of them became for their mothers a living rebuke." Given what he intuits about Sipe, surely Randall might consider the possibility that these mothers are dispatching their daughters to protect them from fathers or stepfathers, unless Randall finds it uncomfortable to consider that possibility in his own case.

5. NIGHT TERRORS (PP. 219-237)

Wallace now has Napier describe the environment and procedures at the sleep clinic (which Hope says has "a somewhat 'dreamy' or dream-like" atmosphere) and begin to describe the meeting in which the Napiers are given a diagnosis. Sexual symbols and imagery continue. The "assigned Somnologist" is Dr. Paphian, named for Paphos, a city sacred to Aphrodite. The adjective "paphian" (meaning "erotic") is used on p. 230 to describe "the young, forbiddingly nubile" technician. This technician is symbolic of Audrey, just as the Medical administrator "with chloasmatic or pre-cancerous lesions on the backs of his hands" is symbolic of Sipe, whose forehead's lesions are referenced on p. 196 and whose hands are referenced as "escharotic or flaky" on p. 195 and as "well freckled" in the rape image of p. 214. Randall also has an erection, first documented on p. 229.

To underscore the fact that the resolution of the Napiers' case is not the primary concern of the narrative and that objective facts do not necessarily resolve arguments, Wallace convolutes the sleep clinic's diagnosis. First, it turns out that Randall was indeed snoring. Then it is revealed that Hope had been dreaming just before she accused Randall of snoring. But then the Somnologist claims that since Randall was snoring at the same time Hope dreamed he was snoring, her accusations "while based on (in his terms) 'interior, dreamed experience' as opposed to 'exterior sensory input,' nonetheless were, in a Medical or scientific sense, 'technically' correct." (Hope asks whether Randall could have been dreaming he was awake, which would account for his "sincere or heartfelt 'denials' of having been asleep," but Randall, repeating the Somnologist's explanation, responds that he could not have been dreaming that he was awake because one cannot be snoring and dreaming at the same time.) And but then when the clinicians cue the videotape to document Randall's snoring immediately prior to Hope's accusations, the audio malfunctions. But the images on the silent video "signified undeniably that sounds and noises of which I had no conscious or 'voluntary' awareness were in fact escaping my mouth—no one with eyes could deny it." Shortly after this realization the dreamer wakes, as reality invades to truncate the dream's denial in mid-sentence.

Far more interesting than the resolution of the marital conflict are the escalating tensions of the dream environment and of intrusions into the dream from outside, often frightening or disturbing. Wallace uses his signature technique of piling on details and digressions (found on every page in this section, some quite long and some nested within other digressions) to approach resolution without reaching it or to represent delay or denial (as of abuse here). As in "The Soul Is

Greg Carlisle

Not a Smithy," what is denied keeps surfacing in the digressions. Acknowledgement or images of abuse have been buried in digressions throughout the narrative; and as the digressions expand here, the idea of abuse is palpable and undeniable, prompting a return to reality at the same time the narrator of the dream is experiencing the reality of the sleep clinic's diagnosis.

As realizations are experienced that will pull the dreamer out of the dream and back to reality, the intrusions from outside are now literally tied to an outside speaker who uses double quotation marks rather than the narrator's conventional single quotation marks. The first instance of an outside intrusion here, *"For God's Sake"* (cf. pp. 198 and 211), is nested two levels down in the first long, 18½-line digression of pp. 221-2.

In another 18½-line digression beginning at the bottom of p. 223 with "Sometimes, nevertheless," Randall describes the suicidal impulses he has while driving that occur for "no apparent or discernible reason." But this parenthetical digression splits almost immediately into a nested em-dash digression in which Randall admits that these impulses are "particularly" associated with the drives he takes to spy on Audrey at college. Note how Randall delays his admission of spying on Audrey with the double-nested digression in brackets at the top of p. 224. In another nested digression near the end of the paragraph, Randall admits that what he feels is "unrelated to the sleep deprivation," but instead of associating the feelings with his yearning for Audrey, he says they "come 'out of nowhere.'" Just after this on p. 224, Randall interrupts his description of Hope's habit of sleeping "as though some great, unwelcome weight were pressing down on her from behind and above" to note that Audrey "often appears to awaken in precisely the same position in which she had originally lost consciousness," indicating that he watched Audrey without her knowledge even before his trips to spy on her in her dorm. The paragraph ends with Randall recounting Hope's charge that their marriage was a "sexless sham, especially now that Audrey was no longer at home to 'preoccupy' me or serve as the 'focus of [my] affections.'"

Just after the Medical administrator is described as having hands like Sipe's on p. 227, loud noises are introduced into the sleep clinic environment. Presumably, the noise is the dreamer's coping mechanism to drown out reminders of Sipe and perhaps also the sleep clinic's diagnosis. But the noise cannot keep two disturbing perceptions from surfacing. The cacophony of sounds includes the "sound of struggles and muffled breathing and a male- or 'Father' figure's whispered grunts and shushing." Randall has a fleeting "vision of a prone female figure wrapped in clear plastic industrial sheeting," surely a reference to Wallace-influence David Lynch's *Twin Peaks*, set in a logging community and featuring in its opening sequence Laura Palmer (who, we eventually discover, was sexually abused and killed by her father), dead and wrapped in plastic (cf. "the ambient smell of freshly cut wood, as well as industrial plastic" on p. 230). The sounds on p. 229 of rain striking a window and on pp. 229 and 230 of a ringing telephone link this section of the narrative to the opening section. Randall recounts that he told his first wife that he didn't want children because he "was afraid of 'repeating the cycle,'" which is resonant with potential fears about Audrey's abuse that could be inferred from her mother Hope's earlier comments to Randall.

Just after Hope is given the reality-changing news that she was asleep when she claims to have heard Randall's snoring at the bottom of p. 230, the dreamer attempts to keep from dealing with that information by initiating a 28½-line digression,

Greg Carlisle

which includes five nested digressions, the third of which is a double-nested command from outside: "*Do stop.*" But just as the content of the marital-conflict narrative has reached a reality-check, so too has the content of the digressions. Randall admits that he fantasizes about storming Audrey's dorm room to "loudly say, avow or cry aloud what may and must never even be remotely thought or 'dreamt of' [unlike, it went without saying, 'Father']." Although no one is allowed to say anything about it, the reality is that Sipe sexually abused Vivian (who acknowledges the abuse) and Hope (who does not acknowledge it when she is awake). The dreamer's despair of this truth prompts the Medical administrator in the dream to "mouth, very distinctly, the word '*Su-i-cide*,' sans any emergent sound" while the cacophony of noise continues.

At the top of p. 232 Hope asks Dr. Paphian for a definitive answer regarding the reality of the Napiers' situation. "At this juncture, the Somnologist . . . now felt absently or 'unconsciously' at his forehead's keratoses, and . . . averred (meaning, the Sleep specialist now averred) that, yes, technically speaking, my wife's accusations" were correct. But the anxiety engendered by the doctor's impending verdict prompts a 29½-line digression omitted by the first ellipsis in the previous sentence and a 3-line digression omitted by the second ellipsis. The first digression opens with Randall positing that Dr. Paphian has misapprehended Randall's expression, which prompts a nested digression about Hope's facial features ("she looked, for a moment, literally decades above and beyond her true age") and a reference to Audrey's "daughterly charms Hope so feared acknowledging were now 'behind' her," which prompts a double-nested digression in which Randall characterizes Hope's removal of Varicose veins as "impotent vanity" and a "'denial' of what had, in fact, long ceased to make any substantive difference." The triple-nested intrusion, "*not start this again my,*" triggers the closure of all the threads of the first digression (the comma at the end of line 6 of p. 233 should be an em-dash instead). The second digression, reversing the progress of the narrative yet again one line later, simply notes that the impending diagnosis constitutes "yet still another . . . reversal." But the nested part of the second digression asserts that "the Somnologist's 'bed side manner' left something to be desired." The Somnologist has just been linked to Sipe by "his forehead's keratoses" (cf. p. 196), and the aide who is about to come in with videos of the Napiers draws a "somewhat affected knuckle across the upper lip" like Sipe (cf. p. 194).

The intrusions and imagery become more disturbing and resonant of abuse as the dreamer rises to consciousness. The last three are "*only hurt a tiny*" and "*Please!*" (this after the videotape is inserted "in to a receptacle or 'slot' or 'hole' in the Monitor's rear") and "*or hurt you if.*" Often in Wallace's work, "The Soul Is Not a Smithy" included, silence is associated with fear or terror. As the relevant part of the videotape of the sleeping Napiers is cued, "all exterior or extraneous noise" ceases, "producing a sudden and somewhat dramatic or unsettling silence." This is also the point at which "no audible sound" can be heard on the videotape playback. Randall references "masturbating with [Audrey's] saffron scented under-garment" and "the wreckage and prone, twisted figures of a vehicular accident" (resonant with his suicidal impulses while driving to spy on Audrey). Watching the videotape, Randall describes his face ("not a face I in any way recognized or 'knew'"), the "variably changing shapes and contortions of [his] unconsciously open mouth" (cf. Sipe's mouth, p. 196), and his "wholly unfamiliar, inhuman, unconscious visage." The "forbidding technician" and Medical administrator, his "hands a mass of amber lesions," "begin to peel their respective faces off." The dream images continue to be torn away as a ray of light, associated with the hallway light that shines under Hope's door as Sipe's "heavy, familiar nocturnal tread" ascends the staircase to her bedroom, shines through Randall's onscreen eye and his facial ex[pression] becomes "'grinningly' familiar and sensual and even predatory," like Sipe's on p. 196.

6. NONE OF THIS IS REAL (P. 237)

Randall's Sipe-like dream face becomes the face the dreamer sees upon awakening. As with "Good Old Neon," it turns out that this story is really about someone other than its narrator, because the only thing we can be certain of now is that the dreamer is Hope. There are several key words and phrases in the dialogue of this last short section that recall earlier intrusions: up, God, hurt you if (cf. *"only hurt a tiny"*), Hope, please, and start . . . this again. Hope awakens at almost 2:04, which is the time on the cued videotape she was just dreaming about. She asks about rain, which was a consistent environmental feature of her dream. The man who wakes her urges her to make an appointment just as Randall does in the dream.

Although roused dreamers are often sleepy and disoriented, Hope's responses are particularly odd if we assume that the content of the dream is taken from Hope's life, which we are apt to do after being immersed in the dream for 47 pages. She asks "am I even married?" and "who's this Audrey?" She addresses the man who woke her, presumably Randall, as "Daddy?" not Father, as in the dream. These questions imply that Hope is in serious denial about her reality. She says, "None of this is real." Why would Hope deny Randall and Audrey in favor of imagining Sipe, the man who abused her? Now that the dream is over, is she denying Sipe's abuse and considering Randall's threat to Audrey an unbearable fact to face?

Hope's dream is prompted by the trauma of her abuse. Note that in the dream, it is always Hope who wakes Randall. Here someone wakes Hope instead. What if Hope's attempt to escape Sipe's abuse is to fall so far into the oblivion of sleep that Sipe won't be able to rouse and rape her? What if the man who wakes Hope is indeed Sipe (she asks, "What's wrong with your mouth?") and her questions about the fictional Randall and Audrey are just part of her disoriented transition from dream to reality? The man orders her to "lie back down." Perhaps the statement "You are my wife" is a signal from Sipe to Hope of the role she is expected to play here in the middle of the night. Right after that, Hope says "None of this is real," which is perhaps a coping mechanism to get her through what is about to happen to her again. The young, traumatized Hope feels so trapped by Sipe that she can't escape him even in her dreams. She tries to fantasize about an adult future away from him ("she looked, for a moment, literally decades above and beyond her true age"), but in that fantasy her daughter has a potentially abusive stepfather, too. Her dream husband seeks out Sipe to make use of Sipe's "paternal influence." She cannot envision an adult sexual relationship; there are no womanly charms, only daughterly charms. Hope's only romantic fantasy in the dream is of riding with Sipe as a girl (p. 197). The intrusions are both Sipe forcibly rousing her and her own memories of previous rapes. She hears Sipe's grunting as industrial noise. As desperately as she tries to deny and escape her abuse, she (as Randall in the dream) realizes "undeniably that sounds and noises of which I had no conscious or 'voluntary' awareness were escaping my throat and mouth" as Sipe clamps his hand over her (p. 214). This would seem the likeliest interpretation of the story, except that Sipe would just make an appointment for Hope rather than ask, "When are we going to make that appointment?" That sounds more like Randall.

Greg Carlisle

It is apt that Wallace chose this as the title story of the collection, documenting as it does the most severe case of oblivion in the book. And the oblivion is associated with Hope's denial, not her dream (see Figure 9). As our denial becomes more fierce and desperate, we become more obsessive and fall deeper into oblivion. The obsessive digressions of this story are not postmodern gimmickry but rather serve to make us closer to Hope. We feel (although perhaps not until a second reading) the obsession and desperation of her thought processes in a way that traditional narratives cannot make us feel.

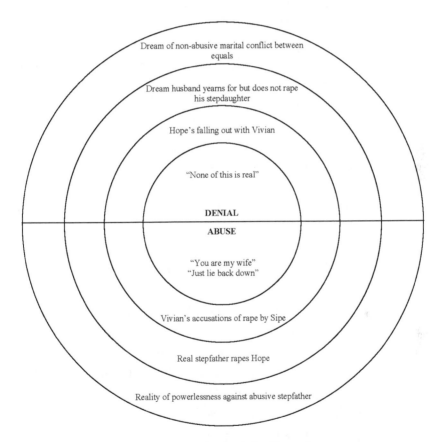

Figure 9. Hope's denial of her abuse

The greatest oblivion comes from not knowing whether our perceptions are of reality or of fantasy. Are we awake or dreaming? Are we interpreting reality accurately? We can't know absolutely. Like the child in "Incarnations of Burned Children," we can't blame Hope for choosing oblivion as a coping mechanism. But escape from oblivion into awareness is prompted not by absolute, objective facts (such as those provided by the sleep clinic's diagnosis) but by choice and belief free of isolation and denial (cf. Hope's sister Vivian's choices and beliefs, which are worthy of consideration whether they are real or only dreamt of by Hope), because what is denied will haunt us and spur further oblivion.

There are a few instances of horrific child abuse in *Infinite Jest* (cf. also Joelle's father's inappropriate yearnings for her). Hope is in worse shape than the abused AA speaker and Matty Pemulis in *Infinite Jest*, because she does not acknowledge her abuse as her sister Vivian may or may not have done. But what is Hope to do? What choices does she have the power to make? What should she believe? Short of reporting abuse to authorities whose protection is dependent on proof that the victim may not be able to provide, is acknowledging the abuse all a victim can or should do? In *The Pale King*, Toni Ware not only acknowledges her abuse, she avenges herself against her abusers and outwits her potential abusers. She can be vicious and vengeful; but she is not in denial, and she is not afraid. And although she seriously threatens a neighbor undeserving of those threats and perpetrates elaborate unsettling pranks, she also is able to interact and work with people as long as they respect her and are willing to abide by her terms. Although she is sometimes violently unfair, surely we can understand why she chooses to be. And surely we prefer Toni's confidence to Hope's despair, so potent that she yearns for suicide in her dreams.

Greg Carlisle

The Suffering Channel

In this final story, Wallace calls pointed attention to the
motto "consciousness is nature's nightmare" (pp. 282, 328), a
comment on the root cause of our oblivion. To be conscious of
ourselves as vulnerable creatures induces suffering, but we are
conscious creatures by nature; and therefore (borrowing
Buddhist phrasing) all life is suffering. To allay this
consciousness-induced suffering we have at least four options,
three of which lead to the various kinds of oblivion experienced
by the characters in this story. We can actively shut down or
passively shut out: a lack of attention in which our suffering is
denied. We can obsess and drive ourselves to hyperactivity,
overloading ourselves with stimuli: a saturation of attention in
which our suffering can be overlooked or buried. We can
channel the suffering and keep it at a distance, witnessing for
example images of others' suffering via a screen that allows us
to countenance our common suffering and loneliness but does
not alleviate that suffering and loneliness: attention without
presence, a kind of emotional limbo. The difficult option is to
experience and acknowledge our common vulnerability and
suffering, accepting the fear and the responsibility as well as the
joy and the reward that are all wrapped up in risking
unmediated human contact, in listening without an agenda:
present attention that minimizes the nightmare of self-
conscious oblivion.

Present attention means focusing on and interacting
with another for whom you are there (present) but also means
collapsing the linear progression of past, present, and future
into the now (the present), which takes us into the territory of
the infinite. Major Wallace-influence Ludwig Wittgenstein
wrote, "If by eternity is understood not endless temporal

duration but timelessness, then he lives eternally who lives in the present" (*Tractatus Logico-Philosophicus*, 6.4311). As we've seen throughout this collection and most of his other fiction, too, Wallace crafts an eternal present in two ways. First, he amasses a multi-page deluge of details that approach but never reach a crisis moment, analogous to a mathematical function that tends to infinity as its independent variable approaches a particular value or limit (cf. Carlisle, *SR* 33-37). Second, his narratives are non-linear, moving fluidly back and forth, continually making reference to past, present, and future events.

1. Toll Call

The first chapter of this story primarily documents a phone call, highlighting the fact that we routinely communicate at a distance. Our preference for communicative distance is an indicator of the power of conversation: an exchange with the potential to take its toll on participants who risk being significantly influenced by each other.

1.1. Irksome and out of character (pp. 238-242)

Again we join Wallace's narrative already in progress (no need for exposition in the eternal present) with "But they're shit" on p. 238. Skip Atwater is on the phone with his associate editor at *Style* magazine after originally dialing his intern, Laurel Manderley, to whom Atwater will be returned for "the subsequent debriefing" of the middle portion of the call currently being documented. The narrator uses acronyms like "BSG" and words like "shades" on pages 238 and 244 respectively but doesn't identify their meaning to us until pages 296 and 297 respectively (no need for intrusive expositional definitions in the eternal present). We learn that it is now "early in the afternoon of 1 July 2001" and then that "*Style*'s editorial offices [are] on the sixteenth floor of 1 World Trade Center in New York," which introduces a future-influenced tension on the present moment.

The associate editor's opening line is in reference to the "[e]xquisite pieces of art" that come "[a]lready fully formed" out of Brint Moltke, the subject of a pitch that the associate editor finds "irksome and out of character for Atwater, who was normally a consummate pro, and knew quite well the shape of the terrain that *Style*'s WHAT IN THE WORLD feature covered." Atwater believes that the associate editor would back the pitch if he "could see the results. The pieces themselves": if the associate editor were there instead of at a distance. At this point the narrative of the toll call is put on hold for almost a page and a half while we are given details about the Holiday Inn restaurant where Atwater is eating with the Moltkes and about Atwater himself, including that Atwater's "periods of self exhortation at mirrors [cf. Terry Schmidt's self-flagellation at his mirror, pp. 33-4] were usually the only time he was fully conscious of the thing that he did with his fist." On p. 239, we learned that Atwater "sometimes unconsciously" moved his fist "up and down in time to his stressed syllables" and of other things about which he was or wasn't attentive.

Just as Skip returns from his phone call and reinitiates contact with the Moltkes by misrepresenting his associate editor . . .

1.2 THINGS PEOPLE DON'T WANT TO BE REMINDED OF (PP. 242-246)

. . . Skip's narrative skips back to the toll call, pointedly indicated by both the back-arrow section-header and by the text of the first four lines of this section. The associate editor reminds Skip that Skip is already working on a "dubious" piece on "The Suffering Channel, a wide grid cable venture that

Atwater had gotten Laurel Manderley to do an end run and pitch directly to the editor's head intern for WHAT IN THE WORLD," one Ellen Bactrian, "who was not only the associate editor's right hand but who was known to have the ear of someone high" on the staff of Mrs. Anger, "Executive Editor of *Style* and the magazine's point man with respect to its parent company." "As with institutional politics everywhere, the whole thing got very involved" (cf. "Mr. Squishy").

Atwater defends Moltke's pieces to the assistant editor by citing the universality of "personal experience with shit." At which point, Wallace jumps seamlessly to the final third of the toll call and has Manderley counter Atwater's implied restatement of his defense with "But personal *private* experience. . . . It's one of the things people don't want to be reminded of." Wallace reminds us of a looming future event by having the associate editor hypothesize pitching Atwater's piece for 10 September 2001 and by having the narrator inform us that Manderley will survive "the tragedy by which *Style* would enter history two months hence." Atwater continues to champion the artistic merit of Moltke's pieces, citing "transfiguration of disgust" as the "upbeat angle" for his journalistic piece about them.

We are also reminded that Atwater "was rarely aware of the up and down fist thing," "one of several lacunae or blind spots in Atwater's self concept." Skip was once told that he had "an insufficient sense of the tragic" "at an age when that sort of thing sank deep out of sight in the psyche and became part of your core understanding of who you are." Laurel was once told that her essays had "a tin ear and cozening tone of unearned confidence, which had immediately become dark parts of her own self concept." Although Skip shares with Laurel "pictures of the four year old schipperke mixes who were his pride and joy," he trusts her in part because he does not think she could "ever be any kind of rival for Atwater's salaryman position at *Style*."

2. DEEP BACKGROUND

As a journalist, Skip is tasked to provide deep background on his subjects, and this chapter calls attention to Skip's journalistic process. Additionally, the narrator weaves into Skip's background on the Moltkes background on Skip and Skip's work environment.

2.1 THE STANDARD MIDWEST ATTITUDE (PP. 246-248)

The narrative now moves back to Skip's initial meeting with the Moltkes earlier in the day of 1 July 2001 in their half of a rented duplex in Indiana, Skip's "native area" (p. 252). The narrator notes that you can see an Indiana storm "coming from half a state away." While you are experiencing the suffocating heat of the present, the storm of the future (which will hit in Chapter 3) is in your sight. Interspersed with details of the Moltkes' Midwest neighborhood and home and appearance and of Skip's memories of childhood (the past alive in the present) are details mysterious and portentous. Brint Moltke works for Roto Rooter; should that raise any suspicions about the source of his artwork? There is an "odd stain or watermark" on the "wall that the Moltkes shared with the duplex's other side." Brint, like Skip, has a hand thing: his "thumbs and forefingers formed a perfect lap level circle, which Moltke held or rather somehow directed before him like an aperture or target." Brint, like Skip most of the time, "appeared to be unaware of this habit." As in *Infinite Jest*, Wallace signals unease with hunched postures, soul-disturbing smiles, reference to "the stuff of nightmares," and bird omens (if the "catalogue clock" bird of p. 247 and the "dead" birds in the paintings of p. 252 count as birds). Skip's thoughts in the brief interval (the eternal present) between his initial prompt for a description of the artist's process on p. 247 and his subsequent prompt span five pages.

2.2 NEAR TESTAMENTAL AWE AND DREAD (PP. 248-249)

Examples of "the various leveling traditions and shticks and reversals of protocol [at] *Style*'s parties and corporate celebrations" are considered. The "effect on morale and esprit" of "Mrs. Anger's annual essay at self parody" "would be difficult to convey," given her status as "a figure of near testamental awe and dread" the "rest of the publishing year." Brief but impressive background on Mrs. Anger is noted.

2.3 RETURNING TO ONE'S NATIVE AREA (PP. 250-252)

In contrast to "the sucking cheeks and starved eyes of Manhattan's women" is Mrs. Amber Moltke, "less a person than a vista, a quarter ton of sheer Midwest pulchritude." Brint Moltke's fixed smile prompts a memory of the "grimace which presaged [Skip's father's] massive infarction" and the subsequent "inability to move" experienced by "little Virgil" ("Skip's true given name") and "his twin brother." Skip "was unaware that the cadences of his speech had already changed" upon return to his "native area." After "a three beat pause," a third verbal prompt from Skip (curious "to know how you do it"), another "stilted pause," and a physical prompt from Amber, the artist says of his process, "I'm not sure."

2.4 SOME KIND OF UNCONSCIOUS VISIBLE CODE (PP. 253-255)

Skip continues to make notes for potential use in his piece, considering that Brint's "digital waist level circle or aperture or lens or target or orifice or void" was "definitely the sort of tic or gesture that meant something," perhaps "some kind of unconscious visible code." Brint's incessant smile prompts yet another disturbing memory from Skip's youth.

2.5 OMITTED THROUGH OVERSIGHT (P. 255)

When Skip reviews his notes, he will notice that context for use of the adjective Willkie (p. 253) is needed for readers outside Indiana. This 3-line section and the next section prompt us to view the narration of this chapter through the lens of Skip's notes. This narrative technique recalls a two-line section that details an omission from the section that preceded it in *Infinite Jest.* (*IJ* 127).

2.6 HIS STRANGE AND AMBIVALENT GIFT (PP. 255-256)

Amber asks aggressive questions of Skip, and after Amber's "inaudible counsel" with Brint, Skip is able to record "Moltke's own first person account of how his strange and ambivalent gift had first come to light." Later, in his hotel room, after "applying crude first aid to his left knee" (a result of another instance of Amber's aggression to be documented in Chapter 3), Skip transcribes Brint's anecdote in his notebook, using bracketed text to sanitize it, giving readers a visual representation of both original anecdote and redaction at the same time.

3. UNIVERSAL CONFLICT

Amid Skip's personal conflicts over his sense of himself as a journalist vs. a writer of fluff pieces and over his journalistic ethics vs. his interaction with Mrs. Moltke, Wallace explores a wealth of fundamental anxieties and conflicts born of the (self-) consciousness that is our common nightmare: workplace status, public vulnerability, unrequited attraction, inherent shyness vs. expressive impulse, spiritual yearning vs. base instinct, and the "conflict between the subjective centrality of our own lives versus our awareness of its objective insignificance."

3.1 AN IMPENDING STORM (PP. 256-257)

After his initial meeting with them in their half of the duplex (Chapter 2), Skip takes the Moltkes to the restaurant in the Mount Carmel Holiday Inn (Chapter 1). Unable to fax pictures of Brint's work there, Skip now takes the Moltkes back home. The Moltkes have boxed up food for "a dog [Skip]'d seen no sign of," and blinds "that had been open on the duplex's other side were now closed, though there was still no vehicle in that side's drive." Amber suggests that she and Skip take his rental car to the nearest Kinko's, a dozen miles east in the nearby community of Scipio, and fax the pictures from there. The distant storm seen in Chapter 2 is now impending. Skip's "fear of the region's weather was amply justified by childhood experience," and for a while he sat "paralyzed with indecision" (cf. Skip's childhood inability to move after his father's infarction on p. 251; paralysis caused by indecision is a recurring motif in *Infinite Jest*).

3.2 CERTAIN PERSONAL LINES AND BOUNDARIES (PP. 257-258)

Skip's indecision triggers a memory of when Laurel confided to him that in Ellen Bactrian's "opinion Skip Atwater was not really quite as spontaneous a person as he liked to seem." Now fearing Bactrian (cf. p. 246), in part because her opinion of him might be true, Skip sometimes "used Lauren's guilt over her indiscretion to get her to do things or to use her personal connections with Ellen Bactrian in ways that weren't altogether right or appropriate" (cf. the "end run" of p. 243). Lauren "accepted it as a painful lesson in respecting certain personal lines and boundaries."

Greg Carlisle

3.3 Coiled slightly, detached (pp. 258-259)

Clearly Skip eventually makes a decision, because he sends Laurel images of Brint's artwork that—in a process analogous to the process of the artwork's creation—emerge, coil, detach, and float from the trayless fax machine he uses back in New York.

3.4 A brief, eerie stillness (pp. 259-260)

Between Scipio and Mount Carmel, the storm hits, and Amber navigates Skip "through a murine succession of rural roads and even smaller roads off those roads" until they arrive at "a kind of crude mesa" overlooking factory lights that "at night were an attraction countywide." It is here that the narrative will be anchored for the rest of Chapter 3. Amber's enormous size and fair skin are again detailed. Because of her susceptibility to sunburn, Amber's umbrella "was not for rain." Skip recalls Brint opening the umbrella for Amber before she even got out of Skip's car in their driveway. "In the light of the storm she seemed to glow."

3.5 An uncomfortable silence (pp. 260-267)

The arrow heading signifies a jump forward to the Monday 2 July working lunch attended by many of "*Style*'s upper echelon interns," including Laurel Manderley. A signature motif of *Infinite Jest* is adult regression to infantile behavior. Here, the "interns all still possessed the lilting inflections and vaguely outraged facial expressions of adolescence" (and one intern uses the phrase "big potty"), which contrast with their adult manners, clipped speech, and coordinated ensembles. Because this is a gathering of fashion-conscious people, the narrator naturally provides specific details of the interns' fashion choices throughout this section. Skip's pitch for the "miraculous poo story" prompts several poo stories from the interns (the first of which "appeared to strike some kind of common chord or nerve"), justifying Skip's claim for the widespread appeal of the piece. The stories—which address gender, culture, and literature as well as personal experience (or second-hand accounts of personal experience)—end up being more about human vulnerability and loneliness than about poo. The interns' storytelling brings the past to bear on the present, and the narrator's assertion that some of the "personal background information laid on the table . . . would alter various power constellations in subtle ways that would not even emerge until work on the 10 September issue commenced later in the month" brings the future to bear on the present. Silence, which brings the present to bear on the present, is significant throughout the section.

The first story is told by "an editorial intern in a charcoal gray Yamamoto pantsuit." She relates "an anecdote of her fiancé's," told in a mutual sharing "of their sexual histories as a condition of maximal openness and trust in their upcoming marriage" (cf. the paean to true marriage in "Mr. Squishy," pp. 31-2). The story describes a "beautiful and widely desired" girl who, "according to the fiancé later," farted while receiving oral sex from the fiancé, a significant illusion-shattering moment for the fiancé who is now "almost unnaturally comfortable with his body and bodies in general and their private functions." Wallace implies here that even base or surface-level human behavior, from flatulence to fashion, has potential significance. The intern's fiancé's anecdote inspires a fit of laughter, after which "there was a brief inbent communal silence while the interns . . . tried to suss out just why they had all laughed and what was so funny." After dry cleaning, Yamamoto's fabrics "never lay or hung or felt quite so perfect," "so there was always a kernel of

Greg Carlisle

tragedy to the pleasure of wearing Yamamoto, which may have been a deeper part of its value."

One of Laurel Manderley's roommates relates a story her therapist told in which the therapist's future wife asked him to leave her apartment because she had "to take a dump," prompting the therapist to realize "that he loved and respected this woman for baring to him so nakedly the insecurity she had been feeling" and that this "was the first time in quite a long time he had not felt deeply and painfully alone." After this story, we learn that Laurel has received an "unannounced overnight package" and that Skip currently is "commuting to Chicago" as expected (for his piece on The Suffering Channel).

Roundtable discussions about the differences in German, French, and US toilet-hole placement (front, back, and middle, respectively) and about "intergender bathroom habits and the various small traumas of cohabitation" follow. Discussion of the marital convention of ignoring a fart prompts this exchange:

"The silence communicates some kind of unease about it."

"A conspiracy of silence."

One of the diners says that her parents called a fart "an intruder," prompting Laurel to get an idea (to intrude into Bactrian's office with the contents of the overnight package, cf. p. 280).

A circulation intern who no one felt they knew very well and "who usually barely said a word at the working lunches" is the only intern to tell her own story (not her fiancé's, not her therapist's). It is the only story at the lunch in which the protagonist is alone. It is an oddly poignant, vulnerable story that begins with the circulation intern, also named Laurel, asking the other interns, "You know, did anybody when they were little ever have this thing where you think of your shit as sort of like your baby . . . ?" It is followed by "an uncomfortable silence."

3.6 Wounded inside (pp. 267-271)

The back-arrow heading signals our return to Skip and Amber, "parked at the little road's terminus" on the stormy afternoon of Sunday 1 July. Amber turns off Skip's tape recorder, making "liberal contact with his knee on either side," and reveals horrific "background facts" about Brint's childhood abuse, the major cause of his extreme shyness. Like the intern's therapist's wife, Brint "can't do his business if there's somebody even there. In the house." On the phone earlier, Laurel had asserted that, given Brint's shyness, what "didn't yet add up for her in the story was how the stuff got seen in the first place." In the full paragraph on p. 271, Skip's instinct says this is "the universalizing element" of the piece: "the conflict between Moltke's extreme personal shyness and need for privacy on the one hand versus his involuntary need to express what lay inside him through some type of personal expression or art. Everyone experienced this conflict on some level." In the paragraph preceding that one, though, Skip recalls beating his chest in the men's room after a performance review in which "the assistant city editor who'd hired him" characterized Skip "as being polished but about two inches deep" and recalls admitting to himself that he "had no innate sense of tragedy or preterition or complex binds or any of the things that made human beings' misfortunes significant to one another." Skip's instincts in the paragraph that follows on p. 271 are at odds with this assessment of himself. Skip, now stuffed up and mouth breathing due to the storm, looks "even more childlike" and recalls that Lauren Bacall's voice "affected one's nervous system in profound ways, as a child" (cf. the voice of *Infinite Jest*'s Madame Psychosis).

Wallace enjoys planting phrases that appear to be clues to something significant but that then turn out to be red herrings that his readers tend to see as clues they haven't figured out yet instead of red herrings. References to the other half of the Moltkes' duplex and to Skip's twin earlier are in this clue-or-red-herring category as is the reference to Skip's reaction to the mention of church at the bottom of p. 268 here. Wallace also places section breaks in the narrative just before crisis moments are reached. Here Skip (who "tended to be extremely keyed up and ambivalent in any type of sexually charged situation") is just about to commit the error (Skip realizes the error "in retrospect") of "asking a centrally important question before he was certain just what answer would advance the interests of the piece." As the narrative progresses it's never made explicitly clear to what question the narrator refers.

3.7 A SINGLE GREAT ALL DEVOURING EYE (PP. 272-273)

Also on Sunday 1 July, cable mogul R. Vaughn Corliss awakes from his tortured sleep—"pirate disks" of which exist and of which *Style*'s parent company are aware—and begins his "invariant" morning routine. Skip, who will drive to Chicago to interview Corliss about The Suffering Channel tomorrow, "had gotten, after a brief and highly structured interface with Corliss for a WITW piece on the All Ads cable channel in 1999, [the sense] that the producer's reclusive, eccentric persona was a conscious performance or imitation."

3.8 A BIT INVASIVE (PP. 273-280)

Skip and Amber, now "breathing each other's air," continue to discuss Brint's shyness. Skip warns that "*Style* is about as public as you can get," prompting Amber's "Well, except for TV." (She says this just after a narrative insert about the cable mogul Skip will interview tomorrow.) Skip delicately asserts the necessity of authenticity tests and seeks confirmation of Brint's willingness to endure invasion of privacy and "personal exposure."

Wallace continues to thread several of his interrelated signature motifs through this story: the fluidity of time, the recall of childhood experience, the lure of the mysterious, and the selectivity of awareness. Reference here is made to later "editorial wrangling over [the] typeset version" of Skip's piece, to "Indiana's refusal to participate in Daylight Savings Time," to the photos Skip faxed earlier (pp. 258-9), and to Skip's childhood; during which he attended a county fair, gained knowledge of "the slight squeaks and pops" made by the moving parts of a "foundation garment," and experienced sensitivity "about his ears' size and hue." The context of Skip's foundation-garment knowledge is a mystery, as are Indiana's mounds and Skip's physical tics. "He had unconsciously begun to do the thing with his fist again," and "neither party commented on" Skip's involuntary "all body shiver." "Unbeknownst" to Skip, the tires on Amber's side "were now sunk in mud almost to the valves. What he felt as an occult force rotating him up and over" toward Amber was "simple gravity."

Amber says of Brint's willingness that "he'll do it for me, Skip. Because I say." Then Amber dares Skip to ask her why she'd "want my husband known for his shit," because she knows that's why Skip's "here in the first place. That it's his shit." And an attention-getter like that of course prompts a section break for Wallace.

3.9 No warning whatsoever (p. 280)

The jump-forward arrow takes us back to Laurel Manderley on Monday 2 July, executing the idea she had (p. 267) at the working lunch to place the contents of the "unannounced overnight package" (p. 264) she received that morning from the Federal Express in Scipio IN (contents that rendered Sunday's faxed photos from the Kinko's in Scipio "more or less moot or superfluous") "out on Ellen Bactrian's desk before she returned from her dance class." There is a mystery concerning the package (to be discussed on pp. 310-1), which explains why someone would later track down the origin of its specialty shipping involving liquid styrene, which specialty shipping it "turned out that a certain Richmond IN firm did."

3.10 Authenticity tests (pp. 280-281)

The jump-forward arrow takes us on to Tuesday 3 July, after Skip's return from Chicago back to Mount Carmel IN and after the "nerve wracking series of in situ authenticity tests at the artist's home" that Skip warned Amber about and that are not the reason (cf. p. 312) Skip "literally limped back" to the Holiday Inn, where he is now again having a phone conversation with Laurel Manderley in which the following words or phrases (clues, red herrings, and/or thematic motifs) recur: Willkie (about whom journalist Skip Atwater speaks in error), duplex, silence, in retrospect.

3.11 The truth was he'd been moved (pp. 281-282)

The back arrow returns us to Skip and Amber "at or about the height of the thunderstorm" on Sunday 1 July. Although unaware of it, the truth was that Skip had now been "tilted 30 or more degrees." Skip counters the "it's his shit" of p. 280 with "It's more than that" and affirms that "something had happened" when he'd seen the pieces and that he now understood "how people of discernment could say they felt moved and redeemed by serious art." Wallace though, via his narrator in the eternal present, reminds us that the truth may be affected by one's environment. "At the same time, it was also true that Skip Atwater had not been in a sexually charged situation since the previous New Year's annual YMSP2 party's [cf. p. 249] bout of drunken fanny photocopying." Is Skip spiritually moved or just sexually charged or both? Does "unnaturally warm" refer to "the Canon's plexiglass sheet" or "one of the circulation interns' pudenda" or both?

3.12 CONSCIOUSNESS IS NATURE'S NIGHTMARE (P. 282)

Wallace calls heightened attention to cable mogul Corliss's company name (note Skip's use of "verily" 15 lines before "O Verily" is used here) and motto ("which for complicated business reasons appeared on its colophon in Portuguese") with a section of only three lines. The motto is heightened again when it appears in Portuguese as the last paragraph but two of our story. The motto seems more significant than Willkie, subject of the other three-line section on p. 255, but perhaps that section actually calls attention to omission and oversight: nature's nightmare's coin's other side.

3.13 THE MANAGEMENT OF INSIGNIFICANCE (PP. 282-286)

Returning to the question of why she would want her husband known for his shit, Amber tells Skip that she realized that it was a chance for her and Brint to "stand out," to "distinguish themselves from the great huge faceless mass of folks that watched the folks that did stand out," to "be known, to matter," to feel that "it made a difference someplace when they came in" (cf. Terry Schmidt's wish to make a difference in

"Mr. Squishy"). Our time-collapsing narrator informs us that in "retrospect, none of this turned out to be true."

Amber's admission that "she'd somehow known that he was her chance" when she'd first met "the drain technician" "struck Atwater as extremely open and ingenuous and naked. The sheer preterite ugliness of it made its admission almost beautiful, Atwater felt. Bizarrely, it did not occur to him that Amber might be speaking to him as a reporter instead of a fellow person." Presumably any suspicions of fraudulence associated with Brint's working for Roto Rooter as a drain technician will be quelled by the authenticity tests conducted two days hence.

Skip associates Amber's confidences with "the single great informing conflict of the American psyche": the universal "conflict between the subjective centrality of our own lives versus our awareness of its objective insignificance." This "management of insignificance" is a conflict particularly alive "in the paradoxes of audience. It was the feeling that celebrities were your intimate friends, coupled with the inchoate awareness that untold millions of people felt the same way— and that the celebrities themselves did not." In Skip's experience, celebrities functioned "as something more like symbols of themselves." Skip's "fist often stopped altogether when he thought abstractly."

Skip then considers this general American struggle with insignificance, "the world altering pain of accepting one's individual flaws and limitations and the tautological unattainability of our dreams," in terms of his own experiences: "the dim indifference in the eyes of the circulation intern one tries, at the stroke of the true millennium, to share one's ambivalence an'd pain with" (cf. p. 282); the way a medical illustrator, Skip's "one and only serious involvement ever" (cf. p. 271), "had looked at him when he undressed or got out of the shower"; and "the shattering performance review from the *Star*'s assistant city editor" (cf. p. 270).

3.14 RAPID ASCENT (P. 286)

The narrative jumps forward to "Tuesday morning" 3 July. Laurel Manderley carries a "box in her arms" and rides elevators in "rapid ascent" "to the executive offices of *Style* magazine" with Ellen Bactrian, who has "verified that the coast was clear" to intrude into the office of the executive intern with whom she has an informal "commuting routine" (cf. p. 246) in the same way that Laurel had intruded into her office the previous day (cf. p. 280), hoping for the executive intern's rapid assent to greenlight Skip's piece.

3.15 TIPPING POINT (PP. 286-288)

Back in the tilted rental car on Sunday 1 July, Amber confesses "that her deepest and most life informing wish, she realized, was to someday have strangers feel about her mere appearance someplace the way she had felt, inside, about getting to stand near enough to Phillip Spaulding" of *Guiding Light* (during a promotional appearance at Richmond's Galleria Mall "at some past point that Amber didn't specify") to reach out and "touch him if she'd wanted to." (Note that Amber does not name the real actor playing the fictional character.) Skip wishes to record a repetition of the vignette to "hold up shieldlike against the voices in his head that mocked him and said all he really did was write fluff pieces for a magazine most people read in the bathroom." Skip's attempts to retrieve the tape recorder wedged between his knee and Amber's hand were, "in retrospect, evidently [mis]interpreted . . . and apparently had a profound effect on Mrs. Moltke." Skip will find himself in "an involved argument with himself later about whether he had

Greg Carlisle

more accurately *engaged in* or *been subject to* an act of fraternization with a journalistic subject." Skip's hands make "fluttering motions" (an activity associated with terror in *Infinite Jest*) "as they beat ineffectually" at Amber, and "either screams or cries of excitement . . . issue from the tilted vehicle" in which Skip is now engulfed.

4. HUMAN INTEREST

Skip's pieces for a glossy magazine are crafted as light stories about interesting people or cultural phenomena, but often our interests are intertwined with our latent fears and anxieties. We are therefore drawn to stories like those of Brint Moltke or of celebrities in crisis and drawn to images like those of The Suffering Channel, stories and images that allow us to consider—vicariously, safely, from a distance—our common baseness, vulnerability, pain, and anguish.

4.1 SOME HORRIFIC SERIES OF IMPACTS (PP. 288-290)

The next day, Monday 2 July, Skip drives his rental car to Chicago "with the driver's side door bowed dramatically out from inside as if from some horrific series of impacts." Our narrator takes this opportunity to give us background information on O Verily Productions and The Suffering Channel, which began as "just montages of [1200] well known photos involving anguish or pain" running in a loop for eight hours a day: "no sound; no evident ads." Again the absence of sound is associated with horror. The photographs on The Suffering Channel are reminiscent of artistic renderings of pain in *Infinite Jest*: in films like *Kinds of Pain* ("silent") and *Fun with Teeth* ("silent w/ non-human screams and howls") made by *Infinite Jest*'s patriarch James Incandenza (*IJ* 987) and in "paintings by artists with crippling cranio-facial pain about cranio-facial pain" (*IJ* 412, cf. *IJ* 1030n162). Expansion plans for The Suffering Channel include the introduction of video clips and insertion into a wider range of markets. The potential merger of The Suffering Channel's parent company with *Style*'s parent company means that Laurel Manderley recently was able to acquire information about the channel, some of which will be presented in the next section.

Although Wallace used the harrowing image, terrible in any context, of people about to "jump from the window of a burning high-rise" in 1996's *Infinite Jest* (*IJ* 696), there is a heightened post-9/11 unease brought to bear on the image of "Brazilians on the ledge of a burning highrise" here, regardless of the presumed geographic location of the image and of the pre-9/11 narrative date of 2 July 2001. Similar 9/11 images are also significant in the works of Wallace's contemporaries Don DeLillo (*Falling Man*) and J. S. Foer, whose *Extremely Loud and Incredibly Close* ends with a wish (fulfilled by flipping reverse-ordered pages) that a man might fall up. Ken Kalfus's *A Disorder Peculiar to the County* also ends with a poignant fantasy that attempts to channel the suffering of both 9/11 and a failed relationship.

4.2 MOMENTS OF HUMAN ANGUISH (PP. 290-292)

This section presents a portion of a "condidential" email (p. 290, the typo is repeated at the top of p. 291; cf. the channel's conflicting web addresses at p. 289, line 7 and p. 291, line 10) received by Laurel Manderley on 24 June 2001 (presumably being read by someone in the present since the header is a continue arrow and not a back arrow). This narrative technique recalls the email about the bricklayer in *Infinite Jest* (*IJ* 138-40). The email describes the contents of a 15-item sample tape of the "most intense available moments of human anguish." The 11th item's "assessment interview" of a "suicidal

Greg Carlisle

female" recalls Kate Gompert's interview in *Infinite Jest* (*IJ* 68-78). The following objective but delicate statement could refer to the person described in the 14ᵗʰ item: the severity of the patient's burns precludes identification of gender. But note that the format of truncated efficiency and distance that characterizes the items in the email instead yields a blunt, crass, humorous description of a "female (?) burn patient." Note that the ratings for the broadcast of the second loop of images triple the ratings for the broadcast of the first loop in February 2001.

4.3 Twin impulses to approach and recoil (pp. 293-294)

The narrator now picks up from p. 286 the fashion-conscious narrative thread of Laurel Manderley and Ellen Bactrian's 3 July surprise visit to the executive intern's office. Meanwhile Skip, thanks to Laurel's handling of "the whole rental car exchange unpleasantness," boards a flight from Chicago back to Indiana. The executive intern, whose "front teeth emerged and pressed lightly on her lower lip," had "unconsciously assumed" the same position as Skip and Ellen Bactrian and others had upon first seeing Brint's work, a position inspired by "twin impulses to approach and recoil." Those twin impulses and the executive intern's "complex and distended" shadow and the chaotic stasis of her "bicycle wheel's still idly turn[ing]" are all signature tension-inducing narrative techniques that Wallace uses repeatedly in *Infinite Jest*.

4.4 The matrix of violation and exposure (pp. 294-296)

The underside of the desire for intimacy with celebrities is the desire to see in them our own baseness and vulnerability. Corliss dreams of taking "the nascent trend toward absorbing celebrities into the matrix of violation and exposure that was Reality" TV to its logical end: "a channel devoted wholly to images of celebrities shitting." The narrator then makes us privy to Corliss's fantasy shit list, the random and egalitarian nature of which is just as comical as good old Neal's list of things he tried on pp. 142-3.

"Almost no adult remembers the details or psychic fallout of her own toilet training." For trainers and trainees alike, such "denials are basic psychological protection." Laurel's training was "no big deal." Skip's and his brother's "had been early, brutal, and immensely effective—it was actually during toilet training that the elder twin had first learned to pump his left fist in self exhortation." Corliss experienced "unambiguous social consequences [that] motivated him to learn almost immediately what toilets were for and how to use them." Vulnerability makes us so self-conscious and afraid that we combat it with punishment or denial, and the suffering of self-conscious vulnerability is often channeled into an unconscious physical response.

4.5 Big soft glossy (pp. 296-301)

This chapter's motif of providing context and background continues. First, definitions are given for "shades" and "BSG": the "abbreviation stands for big soft glossy, with soft in turn meaning the very most demotic kind of human interest." But the tension between glossy elegance and soft baseness is reiterated in the fact that BSGs like *Style* "were at pains to distinguish themselves from the tabloids, whose target market was wholly different."

We learn the origin of Skip's interest in Brint's work. Again, as with tracking details about the packaging and shipment of the pieces sent to Laurel (p. 280), details of the acquisition of the glass cabinets that held Brint's work at the Franklin County Fair would "[l]ater" be determined by Skip.

Greg Carlisle

Does this indicate a continued quest to determine the authenticity of Brint's pieces?

Lists are again used in this chapter, this time to provide copious examples of Skip's previous stories for *Style*. Buried safely in these lists are documents of Skip's vulnerability: "ears about which he'd been savagely teased as a boy," his feeling "that if not for his schipperkes' love he would simply blow away and dissipate like milkweed," waking to his mother's "sardonic ovation." Two stories are given longer treatment: the murder-witnessing parrot that recalls Waldo the myna bird in *Twin Peaks* and the story of a girl born with a "neurological condition whereby she could not form facial expressions." Recall that Corliss must practice his facial expressions daily (p. 272). In a society where people are prone to gloss over or deny their vulnerability, to refrain from risking expression, there might be an increase in the prevalence of this "neurological condition" in which the girl's "face was a flat staring granite mask."

5. TWIN IMPULSES

The conflict of our social, curious natures with our self-conscious natures often prompts us to experience opposing impulses simultaneously, "both exciting and frightful": to tell or to keep secret, to acknowledge unease or to deny it, to ask for help or to run.

5.1 AN OMINOUS VATIC FEELING (PP. 301-302)

As narrative threads converge to approach a crisis event and the mystery of the Moltkes deepens, this dark chapter is driven by the tension of twin impulses to attraction and repulsion (again, a recurring motif in *Infinite Jest*) and by the fear that what is hidden will be exposed. Upon first seeing the photos faxed by Skip on 1 July, Laurel experienced "twin impulses both to bend and get them and to run as fast as she could" and an "ominous vatic feeling" thereafter. That night, she dreamt she was in the Moltkes' home. At one point "there was a dog standing in the middle of the room." Recall that earlier that day Skip saw the Moltkes "with a Styrofoam box of leavings for a dog he'd seen no sign of" (p. 256). In the dream Laurel experiences an "overwhelming sense of dread" and "a premonition of not just danger but evil" (cf. dreams of a face in the floor, *IJ* 62). There are, somehow, two front doors in the dream, and although Laurel's impulse in the dream is to flee, she also finds herself about to open the other door behind which is "the overwhelming evil." Then she wakes up. She has almost the same dream on 2 July, and fears that if she has the dream again tonight, she'll open the door.

5.2 A DELICATE BALANCE OF PRIVACY AND EXPOSURE (PP. 302-306)

This section occurs on 3 July during the authenticity tests from which Skip had returned in Ch. 3.10 (pp. 280-1). Skip had picked up a photographer and a new rental car at the airport and a portable fax machine en route to Mount Carmel, where an internist joined the pair in the Moltkes' home. Skip, "battered and conflicted and ill at ease in Mrs. Moltke's presence," negotiates to have the internist in the bathroom with Brint. Amber protests, citing "skittish bathroom" habits Brint developed in the wake of his childhood abuse, and the MD's "negotiated station was finally fixed at just outside the bathroom door, to receive the fresh piece ('hot off the griddle' had been the photographer's phrase, which had caused the circle of Moltke's digital mudra to quiver and distend for just a moment)." Another of Skip's ominous "childhood associations" —perhaps a peripheral flicker of something he does not want to remember explicitly—is that "he knew it was the heat of the arc

Greg Carlisle

lights that made the [photographer's] hair cream smell so strong."

The mystery of the Moltkes' neighbor intensifies here as well. Upon arrival at the duplex, Skip noticed that "Moltke's company van was parked in the duplex's other driveway, which bespoke some kind of possible arrangement with the other side's occupant." In the Moltkes' bathroom before the tests, Skip "could see that the wall behind the sink and toilet was part of the same east load bearer that ran along the hallway and sitting room and conjoined the duplex's other side." (Note here that Skip would never "have allowed himself to open the Moltkes' medicine cabinet," unlike a journalist Wallace encountered early in his career; cf. Burn ix-x.) Also mysterious, there are "partial cracks and an odd set of bulges" on the surface of the hallway wall, revealed in the crowded hallway by disarranged photos of the Moltkes' "friends' and relatives' children" and of "the Moltkes themselves as youngsters" (adult regression and infantilism and The Cult of the Infant and childhood abuse are all interrelated motifs in *Infinite Jest*).

Our time-conscious narrator notes that Skip is writing a "piece that would eventually run in *Style* magazine's final issue." In a moment of reflection in the hallway, Skip notes that his knee felt "ignominious" (shameful, despicable). Here Skip is channeling the encompassing, self-conscious shame of his liaison with Amber to a localized area of pain, and the word was perhaps triggered by Skip's other realization: "that at some point he and Amber had ceased even pretending to include the artist" in their negotiations.

5.3 OUTSIDE OF YOU AND VISIBLE (PP. 306-309)

Laurel Manderley and Laurel "the editorial intern who had regaled the previous day's working lunch with the intracunnilingual flatus vignette" await Skip's fax of the results of the authenticity tests. As at the working lunch (Ch. 3.5, pp. 260-7), bodily functions are the topic of discussion. Laurel Manderley notes that with saliva and poo and blood, "as long as it's inside us we don't think about it." Of poo and menstrual blood, the other Laurel says, "It's a waste thing, and disgusting, but it's not wrong that it's all of a sudden outside of you and visible, because the whole point is that it's supposed to get out, it's something you want to get rid of." By analogy, if we articulate the causes of our suffering, then the suffering is outside of us and consciously acknowledged and understood, and we have the potential periodically to rid ourselves of it at least partially. If the suffering moves through hidden channels and presents as physical tics, as it does with Skip's and Brint's hands, it stays inside: we don't see it or think about it consciously. "In some respects, Atwater's various tics and habitual gestures were designed to physicalize his consciousness and to keep him from morbid abstractions" (p. 310) and presumably from morbid recollections as well.

5.4 THE WHOLE THING IS JUST VERY CREEPY (PP. 309-315)

The first part of this section documents the same 3 July post-authenticity-test phone call of Ch. 3.10, pp. 280-1. Skip learns that *Style* will for the first time "conjoin two different pieces in process" (Skip's pieces) with "tomorrow's combined coverage spectacle" in Chicago. The logic underlying this decision will play out in the next section. As in "Oblivion" and elsewhere, Wallace increases the tension of the converging narrative by weaving a sense of mystery and dread into the text, enhanced by attention to sensory details, especially the aural landscape. Wallace evokes the sound of Skip's fist with dactylic prose: Laurel could hear the "whispery whisk of his waist level fist." Skip "had evidently misplaced the remote control" ("the controls on the TV itself were inactive") and now heard "the

Greg Carlisle

base channel where the same fragment of song played over and over and the recorded voice of someone who was not Mrs. Gladys Hine [cf. Ch. 4.5, p. 300] welcomed you to the Mount Carmel Holiday Inn . . . over and over." This repetitive quality recalls Laurel's recurring dream (Ch. 5.1, pp. 301-2). Laurel "later realized" that in this phone conversation she was trying "to communicate her unease about the miraculous poo story without referring to her dream of spatial distortion and creeping evil in the Moltke couple's home." Skip is uneasy throughout this section about the "soul killing" "large framed print of someone's idea of a circus clown's face and head constructed wholly out of vegetables," "but it was bolted or glued and could not be moved." Therefore, this section is concurrent not just with Ch. 3.10 but also with Ch. 2.6, in which Skip, after "applying crude first aid to his left knee, and struggling unsuccessfully to move or reverse the room's excruciating painting," transcribes Brint's account of first discovering his ability (pp. 255-6). Brint's only other direct attempt at communication occurs in the last part of this section.

During the call, Skip suddenly feels "that he might well be working for Laurel Manderley someday," a reversal of his feeling in Ch. 1.2, p. 244. Laurel had only shown Ellen Bactrian the pieces she'd received Monday morning because she thought Skip knew that Amber had sent them. When Laurel notes that "Fed Ex isn't open on Sunday," Skip's "whisking sound stopped." Laurel's "the whole thing is just very creepy" prompts Skip's "You're saying she must have sent the pieces before you'd even called" them for the initial interview late Saturday afternoon. After the phone call, Skip realizes he can't remember "to inquire about the other side of the Moltkes' duplex" even though his "notebook later turned out to include a half dozen" reminders. Wallace moves the portion of the phone call in which the duplex is discussed from this section to Ch. 3.10 to heighten this lapse.

Skip, like Laurel, has experienced unsettling dreams for two nights. Skip has "very little conscious recall of his own dreams" but does remember the "sensation of being somehow immersed in another human being." Ominously, Amber (in whom Skip was immersed two days ago) and Skip's mother are here compared with respect to size, likely an inference of abuse when considered with Skip's other ominous childhood associations throughout the story. Consider too the "childhood legacy" of Skip's sensation, upon experiencing bodily pain, "that he was in fact not a body that occupied space but rather just a bodyshaped area of space itself, impenetrable but empty, with a certain vacuous roaring sensation we tend to associate with empty space." Compare this with the child's coping mechanism at the end of "Incarnations of Burned Children," and note that during the painful event the child "made little fists" (p. 115). Examining his bruised and swollen knee, Skip feels a "distinctive blend of repulsion and fascination" and is reminded of "the way he used to feel at the mirror in the bathroom as a boy, examining his protuberant ears." His aversive reaction to the realization "that the bruising was actually trapped blood leaking from injured blood vessels under the skin" recalls the two Laurels' discussion of the previous section.

Brint's "peculiar little unconscious signifier," "the strange abdominal circle or hole that he formed with his hands," "kept popping unbidden" into Skip's mind. The "hands' circle seemed also a kind of signal, something that the artist perhaps wished to communicate to Atwater but didn't know how or was not even fully aware he wished to," but Skip felt the "strange blank fixed smile" did not "signify anything beyond itself." Given the TV's "repetitive tune and message," the water running at the sink, and the ceaseless roaring of the ice machine next to Skip's room, Skip does not hear a "low knocking at the door" (low volume or low fist placement?) that is presumably Brint's. Presumably Brint, not being received, leaves the message that Skip discovers when he eventually opens his door to get ice. Skip experiences "the ambient noise and chlorine smell of the balcony" ("not the only scent in the balcony's wind") and sees *"HELP ME"* (with "plumb straight underscoring" and "quotation marks sic") just before he steps in it. The design of the message, although "not made of icing," reminds Skip of the "decorative icing on certain parties' cakes of his experience": a birthday cake for him and his twin brother, whose name we now discover to be Rob; and the cake at the YMSP2 '00 party where his openness was met with indifference by the circulation intern (p. 285). Skip "was paralyzed by the twin urges" to examine the message and to run from it. Although clearly significant, "the content of the message was obliterated by the overwhelming fact of its medium," a statement that also applies to programming on The Suffering Channel, the impending appearance on which is surely a source of great anxiety for Brint.

5.5 SYNCHRONIZED DOWN TO THE SMALLEST DETAIL (PP. 315-326)

The back arrow takes us to "midday on Tuesday 3 July" before the authenticity test, a proposed list of specs for which is provided on p. 316, allowing Wallace to employ his oft-used list technique to great comic effect once again. Insight into the logic of "the so called artist's appearance on The Suffering Channel's inaugural tableau vivant thing, all of which had been literally thrown together in hours" (p. 310) is provided, with "the proviso that of course it's all academic until this afternoon's tests check out." The narrator describes a brainstorming session between Ellen Bactrian and Mrs. Anger's executive intern occurring in the fitness center below "the WTC's South Tower." However, near the end of the section, the narrator reveals that the executive intern was actually mitigating Ellen Bactrian's "core insecurity" by bringing her "along slowly and structuring their conversations as brainstorming rather than, for instance, her simply outright telling Ellen Bactrian how the miraculous poo story should be structured so that everyone made out." Instead of outright telling us the reason behind *Style*'s decision, Wallace draws out the narrative to build tension and heighten the significance of the decision, which is simply based on *Style*'s need for "just enough of a prior venue so the story already exists." That way *Style* honors the twin impulses of covering rather than creating controversy while simultaneously giving their readers a scoop. The prospect of the dual story is "both exciting and frightful" (and the executive intern's facial expression during the periods of her elliptical-trainer workout that involve reverse pedaling is "both intent and abstracted").

Another reason the logic of the decision is played out point-by-point is the need to dance around the delicate turf issues engendered by Style's hierarchy. Like the "two editorial interns' movements on the elliptical trainers," the plans for the combined coverage event must be "synchronized down to the smallest detail." The self-conscious political atmosphere at Style is again reflected in the narrator's fashion-consciousness in this section, and our discomfort in the presence of raw honesty and vulnerability is reiterated by having Ellen Bactrian repeat to the executive intern "the anecdote that Laurel Manderley had shared . . . about the DKNY clad circulation intern at lunch telling everybody that she sometimes pretended her waste was a baby" (contrast the interpretation of there being an agenda for sharing the anecdote here on p. 321 with the circulation intern's agenda-less behavior back on p. 267; recall that on p. 267 we

Greg Carlisle

learned that the circulation intern's name is Laurel Rodde and that on p. 261 we learned that "no fewer than five of the interns . . . were named either Laurel or Tara"). Wallace simultaneously has his narrator immerse us in a present conversation to help us understand the stakes at risk for the people who work at Style and but then also undercut the importance of those stakes with brusque, time-collapsed perspective. Two pages after the executive intern's "future seemed literally without limit," the section ends with the assertion that she "had ten weeks to live": from Tuesday 3 July 2001 to Tuesday 11 Sept 2001.

At the point that the brainstorming session intensifies into action items later in the locker room, the executive intern does not face Ellen Bactrian: their "eyes met in the compact's little mirror." The executive intern also distances herself from either Brint or Skip, or both of them, by answering Ellen Bactrian's "But do we know for sure he'll even go for it?" with a dismissive "Who?" But the executive intern has something in common with both men: she channels her suffering into unconscious habits (see Figure 10). She "had had a dark period in preparatory school during which she'd made scores of tiny cuts in the tender skin of her upper arms' insides" (cf. Meredith Rand in *The Pale King* 468). "Those days were now behind her, but they were still part of who the executive intern was." Instead now she has unconscious habits: "she bit gently at her lower lip in concentration" (cf. p. 293) and "pressed the heel of her hand into her forehead when she was thinking especially hard."

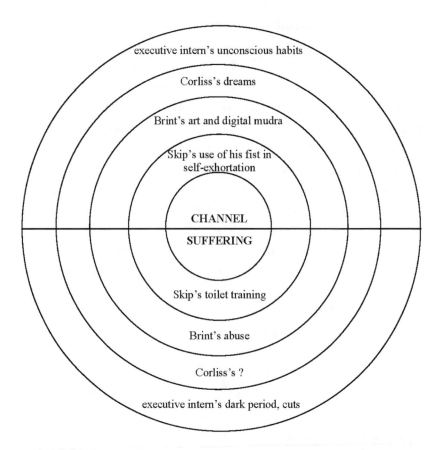

Figure 10. Manifestations of channeled suffering

6. FEEDBACK GLARE

The opinions of others are valuable to us, and yet our self-conscious natures make their feedback analogous to the blinding glare of a "searing and amorphous light." So we attempt to maintain contact while simultaneously dampening that glare: with "darkened glass," with layered thought, with distractions, with distance.

Greg Carlisle

6.1 A RESPECTFUL DISTANCE (P. 326)

On Wednesday morning 4 July, the Moltkes are conveyed to Chicago in a limousine "[h]alf a city block long, white the way cruise ships and bridal gowns are white," which resonates with the "searing and amorphous light" of the "feedback glare" described at the end of the story (p. 329). The limousine and its "darkened glass" distance the Moltkes from the "stolid Caucasian poverty of Mount Carmel" through which they are driven. Although the celebrity-grade limousine suggests to those in Mount Carmel who "were awake to see" it that whoever was inside "saw everything afresh, like coming out of a long coma" (keenly attentive rather than oblivious); it looked to Skip, who trailed "at a respectful distance," "like the hearse of the kind of star for whom the whole world stops dead in its tracks to mourn," which resonates darkly with Amber's wish for the attention of strangers. Inside, there is "a thick glass shield between passenger compartment and driver." The Moltkes face each other, but without meaningful contact: their knees are "almost" touching. Brint's hands, his unconscious signal for help, are "obscured from view by the panels of his new beige sportcoat."

6.2 OBSCENELY ABSTRACT AND DISENGAGED (PP. 326-329)

The Suffering Channel enters "stage three at 8:00 PM CDT on 4 July, ten weeks ahead of schedule, with three tableaux vivant." In the first tableau, viewers will see via split screen a pathology crew's test of a biopsy from a grandmother's pancreatic growth and the grandmother's "face for the whole ten minutes" of the test. Viewers will "get to see the verdict and her reaction to it at the same time." In the second tableau, "Carole Ann Deutsch's widowed father" will be seen listening to selections from over "four hours of high quality audiotape" recovered from the apartment in which his daughter was tortured to death in 1996. In the third tableau, "a video crew will record the real time emergence" of Brint's work into "a clear Lucite commode unit atop a ten foot platform." A "special monitor taking feed from below will give the artist visual access to his own production for the first time." However, TSC viewers will see instead "the artist's face in the act of creation, it's every wince and grimace captured by the special camera hidden within" Brint's monitor and will hear Amber's voiceover documenting Brint's "abusive childhood."

Those covering the event distance themselves from the suffering of the participants by focusing on production issues. The narrative descriptions of the tableaux are intertwined with attention to the auditions and negotiations for the host of the televised segment and to "ticklish problems," "the last minute fix of a production oversight," and "some eleventh hour complication." Narrative attention is paid to fashion in the final paragraph as well. The time-collapsing narrator notes that Skip, "in a move whose judgment was later questioned all up and down the editorial line," devotes attention to the host auditions and to a legal assistant "tasked to the day's multiform permissions and releases."

Just before the narrative shifts to resolution of the tableaux, the motto of O Verily Productions is repeated, this time in Portuguese (cf. p. 282): consciousness is nature's nightmare. The suffering of the tableaux participants is predicated on their self-consciousness. All that is said of the first tableau is "It is, of course, malignant." There is no need to say more because the grandmother suffers more by passively waiting for knowledge about the seriousness of her condition than she does when she gains information upon which she can act or at least experience resolution. Mr. Deutsch seems "less interested in the tapes than in justifying his appearance on the broadcast itself." In an inspired choice of phrase dependent on

Greg Carlisle

capitalization and italics for its dual meaning ("his emergent *Victory*"), Wallace makes us privy to the "dramatic last minute instructions" for the piece Brint is commissioned to create, but as usual, Wallace terminates the narrative just before the crisis event occurs. Wallace closes instead with a powerful metaphor of the problem with which his story is concerned: the intense, all-consuming trap of self-consciousness. Brint's monitor must be kept out of the shot of the ground camera, "since video capture of a camera's own monitor" causes (presumably silent) "feedback glare" in the camera's monitor: "a searing and amorphous light."

Wallace suggests that self-consciousness, and the twin impulses to reach for and to run from those who suffer, is a pervasive American feeling by ending his story on 4 July, ten weeks before 11 September also becomes a significant date in the American consciousness. What would have happened if phase three of The Suffering Channel didn't come early? Would we have been as drawn to The Suffering Channel when the 24-hour news networks became suffering channels in the wake of the 9/11 attacks? Did those events change the way we view suffering? Do we experience more empathy now for those we see suffer at a distance? Would The Suffering Channel seem too crass and exploitative now? It probably would not, given the content of our *Style*-like magazines and our 24-hour news channels and our Reality TV. While the content of our television programming is not yet as horrific as The Suffering Channel, "[t]hey'd laughed at Murdoch in Perth, once, Corliss knew" (p. 296).

One of Wallace's primary themes in both the non-fiction *This Is Water* and in *The Pale King* is the use of present attention and choice to combat the oblivion of self-centeredness, which is called our default setting in *This Is Water* and boredom in *The*

Pale King. The "subjective centrality of our own lives" here (p. 284) is also discussed in *This Is Water* (*TIW* 36-39). The term "well adjusted" is contemplated here (p. 298) and in *This Is Water* (*TIW* 45). Characters in "The Suffering Channel" stay trapped in an inattentive self-consciousness, channeling their suffering into unconscious physical habits. Some characters in *The Pale King* are able to articulate their suffering more objectively, like Chris Fogle recounting the death of his father in §22. Shane Drinion seems best able to pay attention to the suffering of others, characterized by his listening to Meredith Rand's extensive narrative in §46. There are thematic resonances with "The Suffering Channel" in §29 of *The Pale King*, too, which features stories about shit and twin impulses and the vulnerable human being's response to extreme stimuli.

Greg Carlisle

Summary

Oblivion is a condition created by a lack of attention, actively obscuring or passively neglecting stimuli. Oblivion is common because the maintenance of attention at best saps one's strength and at worst induces suffering. Sustained attention is draining or painful because, as the stories in this collection show, reality is complex: it can be manipulated; it is often dull to the point of seeming to be a punishment; it is not always safe; it is based on multiple, simultaneous perspectives; it is not completely within our grasp because of the way we experience language and time; it is not stable because our experience of it is dependent on our subjective sensations and our unreliable memories; and it is subject to radical events beyond our control, events that we would rather not think about. The value of sustained attention is that, although we are independent and our experience of reality is subjective, we simultaneously need other people and believe there is an objective reality outside ourselves. Regardless of that need and that belief, fears and experiences of betrayal and of loss of identity or stability lead us into oblivion. But oblivion removes one from the conversations required for participation in an objective reality and inspires unhealthy, solipsistic mental abstractions. That's the diagnosis in *Oblivion*. Present attention to other people, to concrete details, and to one's lived experience, however painful, is the counterbalance to oblivion. That's the treatment plan suggested in *The Pale King*.

Much of Wallace's fiction grapples with the paradox that our potential for action—our natural instinct for discipline and dedication and service and creative impulses—is necessarily balanced by our tendency toward stasis—our natural instinct for self-protection and self-centered perceptions and mental abstractions—and by the limits of language and of time as we are inclined to experience it. The feeling of being trapped in the routine of day-to-day experience is expressed by Hal in *Infinite Jest* when he asks his trainer "if the pre-match locker room ever gave him a weird feeling, occluded, electric, as if all this had been done and said so many times before it made you feel it was recorded . . . . But also, as a consequence, erasable" (*IJ* 966; cf. "they've all been just here before, just like this, and will be again tomorrow," *IJ* 104). "Another Pioneer" broadens this concept, taking it all the way back to the origins of human civilization and suggesting that history is the routine toggling of human potential and its subsequent erasure, with the flame of human potential passed on—via the inconsistent mechanisms of memory and attention—through storytelling and conversation. And in §25 of *The Pale King*, the boredom of routine—even important routine that yields meaningful results —is represented palpably by the ubiquitous and incessant turning of pages.

Although routine induces boredom, on the other side of that boredom and restlessness and resistance is the bliss of present attention, which is beneficial for everything from improving your tennis game to saving your life. Schtitt says, "Be *here*. Not in bed or shower or over baconschteam, in the mind. Be *here* in total. Is nothing else. . . . Gentlemen: hit tennis balls. Fire at your will. Use a head. You are not arms. Arm in the real tennis is like wheels of vehicles. Not engine" (*IJ* 461). But there is a fine line between outer-directed mental activity and inner-directed mental abstraction. AA counselor Gene M says, "It's the newcomers with some education that are the worst . . . . They identify their whole selves with their head, and the Disease makes its command headquarters in the head" (*IJ* 272). And routine and present attention does not lead immediately to bliss, especially for those who have experienced trauma or

Greg Carlisle

abuse. Gately's heroic dedication to AA's routine activities leads to unbidden memories of his horrific life. Hope is not ready to face those kinds of memories, which routinely attempt to surface in her dreams. The burned child distances himself from his lived experience, trapped in the routine of his "life untenanted, a thing among things, . . . the sun up and down like a yoyo" (p. 116). The narrator of "The Soul Is Not a Smithy" fares better, but still keeps his memories at a distance with mental buffers. In *The Pale King*, Chris Fogle is able to speak directly about his father's horrific death and its effect on his life. But Toni Ware, although present, channels her suffering into threats and extreme practical jokes.

Dedication to causes larger than the self is not a guarantee against self-interest. *Infinite Jest* documents self-interested deviations by tennis acolytes and by recovering addicts from their espoused philosophies and proscribed routines, as well as Marathe's patriotic lectures to Steeply even as he betrays his countrymen. Terry Schmidt wants to make a difference; Neal wants to combat his fraudulence; Skip wants to serve his readers; all are hampered by inner-directed, self-concerned consciousness: nature's nightmare. This is also true of the narrator of "Philosophy and the Mirror of Nature," who, although studious and a good son, is defensive and antisocial. The philosophy of the true heroism of service and the fight against boredom (*TPK* 230-1) inspires the old IRS guard, but that guard is also "driven by self-righteousness, . . . or to work out their own psych stuff . . . . Or else they're drab civil servants in it for security" (*TPK* 546). We learn of this heroic philosophy from Chris Fogle, whom the author character derides as a maundering grandstander (*TPK* 257n3).

The characters in *Infinite Jest* are burdened by consequences of obsessions and addictions that literally weigh them down. Hal and Gately spend much of the last 175 pages of the novel lying down. Alternately, the characters least burdened by self-interest are characterized by levitation, both literal and metaphorical. Lyle warns of the dangers of a weight greater than your own weight (*IJ* 128) and occasionally levitates (*IJ* 700) and manifests as a wraith (*IJ* 933). Mario, who must be held up by a police lock, "floats, for Hal" (*IJ* 315, 316). Characters in *Oblivion* are weighed down by what they don't want to think about and are driven to obscure those burdens. The burned child flees the burden of his trauma and of self-concern, "its self's soul so much vapor aloft" (p. 116). Neal is able to go beyond concerns about his own fraudulence to articulate profound truths about all our limits and insecurities after the expansion of consciousness—the ability to be everywhere like a wraith—that accompanies his death. Characters in *The Pale King* are weighed down by the boredom of their work. The character best able to attend to his work and to the conversation of others is Shane Drinion, who levitates "when his attention is completely on something else" (*TPK* 485). Wallace's notes for the novel also feature examples of people "able to achieve and sustain a certain steady state of concentration, attention, despite what they're doing" (*TPK* 547).

Part of what readers admire about *Infinite Jest* and *The Pale King* is Wallace's ambition: the attempt to coax us out of the complicated mazes of our self-obsessions, of our addictions and our boredom, by first dragging us through them in his vast, sprawling narratives. And while form also reflects content in those longer works, the crucible of his shorter stories inspires in Wallace a profound efficiency. He is able to pack the ambition of a novel into these sharply articulated stories whose form perfectly reflects their content on every page and whose themes hit the reader all-at-once in a neon flash of creativity. Although *Oblivion* has not yet received the level of attention that *Infinite Jest* and *The Pale King* have, some of the finest

Greg Carlisle

revelations of Wallace's craft and of his mission as an artist are there.

Acknowledgments

I want to thank Michael Sheehan and David Hering for invitations to the Wallace events they hosted in 2009, in Tucson and Liverpool respectively. Their commissions kept me writing about Wallace when I thought I was finished, which led to my interest in writing this book.

I want to thank those who read drafts of these analyses. I am especially indebted to Thomas Tracey, whose meticulous review of my commentary on the first four stories greatly improved their clarity.

I want to thank Kyle Ware for another fantastic work of cover art.

And I want to thank John Bucher and Matt Bucher, sources of encouragement and enthusiasm throughout this entire process, even when the book was barely an idea. The positive spirit of online Wallace enthusiasts is also a great motivator. Matt's design aesthetic and editorial skill are again much appreciated.

Works Cited

The page numbers below identify where these sources are referenced in this book.

Burn, Stephen J. "Introduction." *Conversations with David Foster Wallace*. Ed. Stephen J. Burn. Jackson: University Press of Mississippi, 2012. p. 139

Carlisle, Greg. *Elegant Complexity*. Los Angeles/Austin: Sideshow Media Group, 2007. p. 11

— "Wallace's Infinite Fiction." *Sonora Review* 55-56 (2009): 33-37. pp. 31, 116

DeLillo, Don. *Falling Man*. New York: Scribner, 2007. p. 134

— "Informal Remarks from the David Foster Wallace Memorial Service in New York on October 23, 2008." *The Legacy of David Foster Wallace*. Edited by Samuel Cohen and Lee Konstantinou. Iowa City: University of Iowa Press, 2012. p. 72

Foer, Jonathan Safran. *Extremely Loud and Incredibly Close*. Boston: Houghton Mifflin, 2003. p. 134

Gaddis, William. *Agape Agape*. New York: Viking, 2002. p. 68

Joyce, James. *A Portrait of the Artist as a Young Man*. p. 33
The older Stephen Dedalus of Joyce's *Ulysses* is also referenced on p. 44.

Kalfus, Ken. *A Disorder Peculiar to the Country*. New York: Harper Perennial, 2006. p. 134

McCaffery, Larry. "An Expanded Interview with David Foster Wallace." *Conversations with David Foster Wallace*. Ed. Stephen J. Burn. Jackson: University Press of Mississippi, 2012. pp. 29, 89

Oxford American Writer's Thesaurus. Oxford University Press, 2004. pp. 9-10

Roiland, Josh. "Getting Away from It All: The Literary Journalism of David Foster Wallace and Nietzsche's Concept of Oblivion." *The Legacy of David Foster Wallace*. Ed. Samuel Cohen and Lee Konstantinou. Iowa City: University of Iowa Press, 2012. pp. 9-10

Rorty, Richard. *Philosophy and the Mirror of Nature: Thirtieth-Anniversary Edition*. New Jersey: Princeton University Press, 2009. pp. 91-92

Twin Peaks. Created by David Lynch and Mark Frost. ABC Television. 1990-1. pp. 108, 137

Wallace, David Foster. *Infinite Jest*. Boston: Little, Brown, 1996. pp. 9, 11, 30-32, 37-38, 44, 49-50, 52-54, 60-61, 70-71, 73-74, 76-77, 79, 82, 85, 92-93, 101, 114, 119, 121-123, 126, 133-135, 137-138, 151-155

— *Oblivion*. Boston: Little, Brown, 2004.

— *The Pale King*. Boston: Little, Brown, 2011. pp. 9-11, 13, 31-32, 55, 62, 72, 85, 89, 96-97, 114, 145, 149-150, 151-155

— "Solomon Silverfish." *Sonora Review* 55-56 (2009): 67-96. p. 31

— *This Is Water*. Boston: Little, Brown, 2009. pp. 9-10, 32, 78-79, 149-150

Wallace, Sally Foster. *Practically Painless English*. New Jersey: Prentice-Hall, 1980. pp. 99-100

Wild at Heart. Dir. David Lynch. Samuel Goldwyn Company, 1990. p. 44

Wittgenstein, Ludwig. *Tractatus Logico-Philosophicus*. pp. 89, 115-116